5º Grand Picnics

50
P

Grand Picnics

MENUS & RECIPES
for the
BEST PICNIC SITES
around
THE BAY AREA

■

Beverly Levine

Chronicle Books
SAN FRANCISCO

*To my dear husband Charlie, who gallantly
tried all the recipes that appear in this book —
and, more important, those that don't!*

LIBRARY OF CONGRESS CATALOGING
IN PUBLICATION DATA
Levine, Beverly.
50 grand picnics.
Bibliography: p. 178.
Includes index.
1. Picnicking. 2. San Francisco
region (Calif.)—Description
and travel—Guide-books.
3. Picnic grounds—California
—San Francisco region—
Guide-books. I. Title.
II. Title: Fifty grand picnics.
TX823.L48   642'.3   82-1280
ISBN 0-87701-189-3   AACR2

BOOK AND COVER DESIGN
Howard Jacobsen

COMPOSITION
Type by Design

Chronicle Books
870 Market Street
San Francisco,
California 94102

Contents

Picnics for Bird Watchers

Picnics with Music

Picnics with History

Picnics in the Wine Country

Picnics for Pickers

Picnics amid the Flowers

Picnics in the City

Picnics by Lakes & Streams

Introduction

Just the word "picnic" is enough to cheer up anyone who loves to eat outdoors. Whether it's a brown bag lunch outside on the first warm, sunny day of spring, or a full-scale beautiful meal for favorite people, a picnic is a happy event.

As for places to go, no other part of the world offers a greater choice than the San Francisco Bay Area. From carefully manicured gardens to redwood forests, from placid pools and gurgling creeks to rugged seaside cliffs, the variety of terrain and environment is almost inexhaustible. In this book you'll find fifty of the loveliest of these places, suggested menus and recipes for each picnic, and directions for packing and carrying the food.

The Places

The only difficulty in picking the places was in narrowing the choices down to only fifty! In addition to sheer physical beauty, two criteria for the picnic locations were that the spots should not be chronically overcrowded, and that they should offer other things to do besides eating the picnic—though, of course, that's the most important thing! I hope you'll find both old favorites and new places to try.

The Food and Drink

If you just like to stick a peanut butter sandwich in your pocket and head out, I hope you'll keep right on doing it, and that you'll also try some of the menus and recipes offered here. You'll find picnics for tucking into day packs, a few elegant ones that suggest a tablecloth and real wineglasses, and some that require barbecue equipment. Each has instructions for packing up. At the end of this section you'll find check lists so you won't forget anything essential.

Because most Californians enjoy it, a bottle of wine is suggested to go with most of the picnics. Leave your subtle and expensive vintages at home, and bring along a bottle of something simple but tasty. Drinks other that wine are suggested with some picnics where appropriate. I've included coffee with most of the menus because I like it to finish a meal. Naturally, you may want to make some changes in the menus and recipes to suit your picnickers' tastes and appetites. Most of the picnic menus are designed to serve four people.

Equipment

You may carry the food in anything from a supermarket sack to an elegantly fitted-out British picnic hamper, but the following pieces of equipment are well worth having on hand if you like to picnic.

- Two large vacuum bottles, one wide mouthed for soups
- A basket deep enough to hold a chicken and wide enough to accommodate a nine-inch casserole or pie plate. For years I've carried a three-tiered one that works wonderfully, but any basket with a sturdy handle will do.
- A cooler. The lightweight ones with lids that can be frozen to provide the cooling power are handy. For larger picnics, a full-size one that requires ice may be best. The ice can go in self-sealing plastic bags, or can be frozen in clean milk cartons.
- Silverware that can be left in the basket. The disposable plastic type is all right in a pinch, but not really very satisfactory.

- Plates and glasses or cups. I don't object to paper plates, and they certainly make clean-up easier. If you like the convenience of a plastic set, there are amazingly compact ones on the market. Plastic wineglasses and Styrofoam cups are easy to use and throw away.
- A mat or ground cloth. A woven mat kept in the trunk of the car comes in handy for spontaneous outings. If you like to hike, the lightweight folding ground cloths for campers are very useful.
- Plastic containers for food. Two large and three small should do it. Lids work better on round ones, but square ones pack more efficiently.
- Plastic bottle for water. A collapsible one works well.

Any number of other things can come in handy, such as wicker trays to put under the paper plates to give them more stability; enameled stacking containers for hot foods (these come from Mexico); plastic or lacquered trays and containers from Japan; collapsible containers for mustard and catsup; and so on. Good places to shop for picnic accessories are Japanese or Mexican hardware stores, the camping sections of sporting goods stores, or specialty shops such as Taylor & Ng or the Tisket a Tasket in Ghirardelli Square.

Safety and Such

- Most cooked foods can be kept at room temperature for two hours without any problem. If you carry the picnic in a cooler in the car you'll be extra safe.
- Nobody likes a picnic better than your average yellowjacket, and these stinging little pests have ruined more California picnics than ants ever dreamed of. Insect repellent can help, but it won't keep them off your food. It's sometimes useful to make them an offering of a piece of food placed a few yards away (they *love* chicken!) but that is a stop-gap measure. The most effective procedure is

to move. Yellowjackets hang around picnic sites because they are attracted by the food and waste containers, so you can often thwart them by moving away from the picnic tables and setting up on a mat somewhere else. The only sure remedy is to picnic in some season other than summer—we have delightful days all year round!

- ✔ Do learn to recognize poison oak and avoid it. It is everywhere in the Bay Area. If you think you've touched it, have a shower when you get home, and pop all of your clothes in the washing machine right away.
- ✔ Follow the rules of the park you are in, of course, and do stay on trails so as not to destroy natural habitat.
- ✔ Nothing ruins the beauty of a picnic spot faster than litter. I once found a classic piece: a plastic sack that had contained a litter bag. *Don't leave anything behind that you brought with you or this book will disintegrate in your hands!*

Omar Khayyám had the necessary elements for a great picnic very well pegged with his "Book of Verses underneath the Bough,/A Jug of Wine, a Loaf of Bread and Thou/Beside me, singing in the Wilderness. . . ." With these lovely places and tasty menus, you should have no trouble attracting pleasant company to share your outdoor delights, whether they can sing or not. Happy picnicking!

Check Lists for Packing Up

Check List A

- sharp knife
- corkscrew–bottle opener
- napkins

Check List B

EVERYTHING ON CHECK LIST A, PLUS:

- plates (extras for dessert if necessary)
- knives, forks, spoons (extras for dessert if necessary)
- large serving spoon
- glasses for wine or other beverage
- cups for coffee (powdered cream and sugar)
- ground cloth or mat
- small cutting board
- plastic bottle of water

OPTIONAL

- drinks for children
- tablecloth
- insect repellant
- salt shaker

Check List C

EVERYTHING ON CHECK LISTS A AND B, PLUS:

- charcoal
- charcoal starter
- matches
- hot pads
- tongs
- spray bottle
- aluminum foil

OPTIONAL

- your own hibachi or grill (those provided are sometimes pretty grubby)

Picnics
with
a
View

Marin Headlands

1

Take the Alexander Avenue exit from Highway 101 just north of the Golden Gate Bridge. Turn left under 101, following the signs back towards San Francisco. Turn right onto Conzelman Road. Tables, barbecues. Restrooms and water at Rodeo Lagoon.

San Franciscans who feel happiest in sight of the water and within the sound of foghorns will wear smiles (and windbreakers) at Marin Headlands. You're outside the Golden Gate here, and once you're on Conzelman Road, you'll want to stop often to admire the spectacular views out to sea and back through the strait toward the city. The wind is usually fierce here at the top of the cliffs, and the first opportunity to find a sheltered spot to picnic is along the trail to Kirby Cove. Watch for the trail head to your left about half a mile in. Camping is allowed by reservation at the small beach at the bottom of the cliff, so it is often occupied.

Benches near the road mark other good spots to stop for a minute. The old batteries scattered along the way are interesting to explore and can provide some shelter from the wind, but they are a little grim for happy picnicking. For the best spot, continue just past the intersection of the road to Point Bonita with the road to Rodeo Beach. Here, on the left, you'll find a group of picnic tables with barbecues, sheltered by some hardy cypress trees. On a clear day, you'll see the whole western side of the city, with Land's End in the foreground. As you watch, ships will cruise in and out of the harbor, and the fog may creep in and out a bit, too.

If you prefer beach picnicking, continue to Rodeo Beach where you'll find a ranger station and some old Coast Guard buildings. A few tables are located along the lagoon; more are by the ranger station. Or you can cross the wooden bridges to the beach itself and spread out your blanket on the sand. No swimming is permitted here because the water is very rough. Nearby Bird Island looks like a bit of the Mendocino Coast transported south, and hiking trails lead up to more views out over the Pacific.

Wherever you have chosen to picnic, return to 101 via Bunker Road, which goes through a one-way tunnel with traffic controlled by a light that changes every six minutes.

Marin Headlands Chili Warm-Up

CHILI WITH A CHOICE OF TOPPINGS

TORTILLAS

FRESH FRUIT

MEXICAN TEA COOKIES

BEER & COFFEE

CHILI

4 large onions, chopped
6 tablespoons oil
1 tablespoon mustard seed
1½ pounds ground beef
1 tablespoon chili powder
1 teaspoon cumin seed
¼ teaspoon ground cardamom
¼ teaspoon ground cinnamon
One 1-pound can tomatoes, including juice

One 6-ounce can tomato paste
1 cup water
3 cans (1 pound total) kidney beans
Chopped onions
Sour cream
Shredded jack cheese
Lime wedges (optional)
Chopped fresh cilantro (optional)

In a large kettle, cook the onions in the oil, stirring, until soft. Add the mustard seed and cook about 1 minute. Add the ground beef and cook, breaking the meat apart, until lightly browned. Add the remaining ingredients except toppings, breaking the tomatoes into pieces, and cook uncovered, stirring occasionally, for 40 minutes.

Bring chopped onions, sour cream, and shredded jack cheese, in separate small plastic containers with lids, to spoon on top of the chili. Some limes cut in wedges are nice for the chili or to add a few drops of lime juice to the beer. Chopped fresh cilantro is also good if you like the flavor. Serves 4 generously.

MEXICAN TEA COOKIES

½ cup butter, softened
2 tablespoons sugar
Pinch of salt
1 cup sifted all-purpose
   flour

1 teaspoon vanilla
Powdered sugar

Cream the butter and sugar, mixing until fluffy. Add the salt to the flour and blend with the butter and sugar, then add the vanilla. Form into small balls and place on a cookie sheet. Bake at 350°F. for 15 minutes. When cool, roll in powdered sugar. Makes about 30.

Packing Up

TO CHECK LIST B, ADD:

✔ bowls for chili
✔ large spoons

Subtract wineglasses.

COOLER

✔ beer
✔ fruit in a rigid container

BASKET

✔ chili well wrapped in
   newspaper and a towel
✔ tortillas heated and
   wrapped in aluminum
   foil, 4 to a package

✔ coffee in a vacuum bottle
✔ dishes and utensils
✔ cookies in a rigid
   container

At the picnic site, spoon the chili into the bowls, then pass the toppings and the tortillas. Open a beer for everyone. The fruit and cookies can be enjoyed later with coffee, hot from its container. This should be a cozy picnic, as everyone will want to sit on the same side of the table to admire the view.

Coyote Hills Regional Park

2

In Newark, take the Jarvis Avenue exit from Highway 17, go north on Newark Boulevard to Patterson Ranch Road, and follow the signs into the park. Open 8:00 A.M. till dark. Interpretive Visitors' Center open Monday from noon to 4:30 and Tuesday through Sunday from 8:30 to 4:30. Telephone (415) 471-4967. Parking $1.25.

You may not see a coyote at Coyote Hills, but you could find yourself looking down on a hawk as he swoops into the marshland below after prey, and you will surely see a splendid view of the entire Bay: south to the salt evaporation ponds that form its lower expanses, north to Mount Tamalpais and the oil tanks of Richmond, and northeast to Mount Diablo.

On terraces behind the Visitors' Center you'll find shaded picnic tables set on the grass, with good views out over the marshes. (Look alive if the turkey vultures start to circle.) If it's a hot day, you may choose to picnic here, but the best view is up the Red Hill Trail. Though it's only 200 feet in elevation, you'll find a 360-degree view, surely worth the short climb. If it's a clear winter or spring day, the sun will feel welcome as you spread out your ground cloth and prepare to open the lunch.

After the picnic you can visit a shell mound left by the local Indians during their 2,500 years of habitation, hike or bike along the Alameda Creek or Bay View trails, or spend some time bird-watching on the boardwalks out over the marsh. Call the number above to see if any special naturalist programs that would be of interest are planned for the day of your picnic.

Coyote Hills Meat Pastries Collation

MEAT-FILLED PASTRY

PICKLED ONIONS A LA GRECQUE

CRUNCHY GREEN PEA SALAD

SHOESTRING POTATOES

FRESH FRUIT

INDIVIDUALLY WRAPPED MINTS

BEAUJOLAIS OR ZINFANDEL

COFFEE

MEAT-FILLED PASTRY

Coyotes like meat, right? Cooked rabbit or venison is delicious used in this dish, but as those are hard to come by, here it is made with ground beef.

You can use any favorite yeast dough recipe, or use biscuit dough or even a package of crescent refrigerator rolls. For an easy yeast dough pastry, you can use a loaf of frozen bread dough. Let it thaw clear through, then cut it into 8 equal portions and shape them into balls. Let the dough rest, covered, for 30 minutes. Roll each ball of dough into a circle about 5 inches across and place about 2 tablespoons of the following meat filling in the center. Bring the edges of the circle up in thirds, and squeeze the edges together firmly to form a triangular bun with three seams on top.

Put the filled rolls on two greased cookie sheets and let the rolls rise, covered, in a warm place until they are puffy, about 45 minutes. Brush with 2 eggs beaten with 1 tablespoon of water, and sprinkle with sesame or poppy seed. Bake at 400°F. for 18 to 20 minutes. Cool on a rack. Wrap individually for the picnic. Can be frozen. Makes 8.

Filling

¾ pound lean ground beef
1 medium onion, chopped
1 clove garlic, chopped
¾ teaspoon salt
½ teaspoon ground cinnamon
½ teaspoon ground allspice
¼ teaspoon pepper
¼ teaspoon ground cumin
¼ cup beef broth or water flavored with bouillon cube
2 tablespoons sherry or cognac
2 tablespoons minced parsley

Cook the ground beef in a frying pan until it loses its color. Add the onion and garlic, and cook until the onion is limp.

Stir in the spices and broth and cook, stirring, until most of the liquid is evaporated. Add sherry or cognac; stir. Cool, then stir in the parsley.

PICKLED ONIONS À LA GRECQUE

Empty a large jar of pickled onions into a glass bowl or plastic container. Add ¼ cup raisins, ½ teaspoon sugar, ½ teaspoon each tarragon, mustard seed, and pepper, and 1 whole clove. Chill thoroughly. Sprinkle with chopped parsley just before packing. Serves 4.

CRUNCHY GREEN PEA SALAD

One 1-pound package frozen green peas
One 8-ounce can water chestnuts, drained and sliced *or jicama*
2 tablespoons chopped pimiento

⅓ cup sliced green onion
½ cup sliced celery
⅓ cup mayonnaise
1 tablespoon Dijon mustard
½ teaspoon garlic salt
¼ teaspoon pepper

Add froz. peas to saled

~~Cook the peas in boiling water until just tender, drain~~. Rinse with cold water and drain again. In a bowl, combine the peas, chestnuts, pimientos, onion, and celery.

Make a dressing of the remaining ingredients and stir into the salad; cover and chill. Serves 4.

Packing Up

CHECK LIST B

COOLER

- ✔ pickled onions in a plastic container
- ✔ salad in a plastic container
- ✔ fruit in a rigid container
- ✔ mints in a small rigid container

BASKET

- ✔ meat-filled pastries, wrapped in plastic wrap
- ✔ shoestring potatoes
- ✔ wine
- ✔ coffee in a vacuum bottle

At the park, you can transfer the food to day packs for ease of carrying if you like, but it's not very far up the hill. Put the ground cloth on top so that it comes out first. Open the wine and the shoestring potatoes, and give each picnicker a serving of the salad, the onions, and a meat pastry (seconds later). Then prepare to enjoy the view and your Coyote Collation.

Sutro Heights Park 3

In San Francisco just above the Cliff House at the end of Geary Boulevard, or Point Lobos Boulevard and 48th Avenue. Park along the avenue and enter from there. Tables. No restrooms, no barbecues, no water.

San Francisco's former mayor, Adolph Sutro, had an eye for a good building site. Here at Point Lobos he constructed the Sutro Baths, now falling into ruins near the sea; an earlier version of the Cliff House; and, overlooking it all on the top of the cliff, a mansion with a panoramic view. Though nothing remains of the house but the foundation, a stone promenade still looks out at the Great Highway stretching to the south, the seal rocks almost directly below, and the Marin coastline to the north across the Golden Gate.

Sutro was a Populist politically—his famous horizontal mining tunnel in the Sierras was finally financed by the miners, who realized that it would provide them with a great deal more safety than the old vertical type—and he allowed the public to visit the grounds of his house even when he lived here, though in those days you had to park your picnic basket at the gate. Now that the beautiful grounds are part of the Golden Gate National Recreation Area, you may picnic wherever you please.

It's often windy out where the views are best, but there are plenty of sheltered spots back from the water. Pleasant lawns dotted with trees, fountains, statues, and a gazebo create a delightfully restful atmosphere. Near the street, almost concealed in what was once a European-style maze of hedge, are four picnic tables. You can choose one of these, or spread out your blanket anywhere in the grassy, sun-dappled park.

Brunch on Sunday was a tradition at the Sutro mansion, and besides various family members, such distinguished visitors as President Benjamin Harrison and poet Oscar Wilde were guests of Mayor Sutro. So here is a Sutro brunch-picnic in honor of the "Lord of the Comstock."

Sutro Heights Sunday Brunch

SKEWERS OF MELON AND HAM CUBES

FRITTATA

LOX, CREAM CHEESE, AND BAGELS

OTHER BREADS (CROISSANTS, BRIOCHES, FRESH RYE)

APPLE STRUDEL PASTRY

CHAMPAGNE

LOTS OF HOT COFFEE

FRITTATA

½ cup chopped fresh spinach
½ cup chopped onion
2 tablespoons butter
5 eggs
½ cup heavy cream
¼ teaspoon salt
⅛ teaspoon pepper
Chopped parsley
Sliced tomato

Lightly sauté the spinach and onion in the butter. Combine the eggs, cream, salt, and pepper with the vegetables. Preheat a 9-inch-square baking dish, buttered, in a 375°F. oven. When the butter is bubbling, pour in the egg mixture. Bake until puffy and set in the center, about 20 minutes. Decorate with parsley and tomatoes. Serves 6.

APPLE STRUDEL PASTRY

1 sheet puff pastry (half a 17¼-ounce package)
2 cups sliced peeled apples
4 tablespoons sugar
¼ teaspoon ground cinnamon

Let 1 sheet of the puff pastry stand at room temperature 20 or 30 minutes (covered). Place on an ungreased baking sheet and unfold pastry. Arrange apples in layers, overlapping slightly, on top of the pastry. Sprinkle with sugar and cinnamon. Bake at 425°F. for about 20 minutes. Makes 6 servings.

Packing Up

TO CHECK LIST B, ADD:

✓ a server for the frittata

COOLER:

✓ skewers of melon and
ham in a plastic bag (use
small wooden skewers)
✓ lox wrapped in plastic
wrap

✓ cream cheese in a plastic
bag
✓ champagne

BASKET:

✓ frittata in its pan, well
wrapped in newspaper
✓ all the breads wrapped in
plastic wrap
✓ apple strudel pastry, cut
into servings and
wrapped in plastic wrap

✓ coffee in a vacuum bottle
✓ plates and utensils
✓ ground cloth

At the picnic site, put out the ground cloth and the plates and
silverware, and give everyone a skewer of fruit. Serve the frittata, and let everyone help himself to the rest. Don't forget to
drink a toast to Mayor Sutro when you open the champagne.

Clipper Cove, Treasure Island– Yerba Buena   4

---

*From the Bay Bridge, take the Tresure Island exit. Follow
signs toward the Navy Marine Corps Museum. Clipper
Cove is to the right, just before you reach the gate of the
Navy base. Tables, barbecues. No restrooms, no water.
Navy Marine Corps Museum open daily 10 to 3:30; free.
Telephone (415) 781-1775.*

The splendid views of San Francisco and the Bay
enjoyed by the throngs visiting Treasure Island during
the Golden Gate International Exposition in 1939 are

still there to be savored. Most of Yerba Buena and Treasure Island is closed to the public, but thanks to the efforts of the Civilian Conservation Corps, you can picnic at Clipper Cove on Yerba Buena.

Above the cove itself you'll find several picnic tables, one barbecue, and a superb view from the underside of the bridge out over the whole eastern expanse of the Bay. A trail leads down to the cove, and you can carry the picnic there if you prefer to be by the water. When the tide is out, you can walk a little way along the shore. Blackberry bushes, lilac, and nasturtiums give the secluded site at the top an unexpected feeling of being a long way from city bustle.

Before or after the picnic, do drive on down to the Navy Marine Corps Museum, where you can admire the views toward San Francisco from the parking lot, and visit the exhibits inside, which include an immense mural portraying the history of Navy and Marine activities in the Pacific.

Treasure Island Hidden Bounty Meatloaf Fare

BURIED BOUNTY MEATLOAF IN A CRUST

ARTICHOKES WITH HERBED MAYONNAISE

CHILLED CARROTS AMANDINE

BREAD STICKS

FRESH FRUIT

GRENACHE ROSE

COFFEE

**BURIED BOUNTY
MEATLOAF IN A CRUST**

Don't let the length of these instructions deter you; this is no harder to make than standard meatloaf, and it is very impressive to serve. When sliced, the meatloaf will have a gold stripe of carrot and green stripe of beans.

1 medium carrot	¼ cup grated onion
1 handful of fresh or frozen green beans	1 teaspoon salt
	⅛ teaspoon pepper
⅔ cup dry bread crumbs	½ teaspoon dried
1 cup milk	sage
1½ pounds lean ground beef	1 package (6) frozen puff-pastry shells
2 eggs, beaten	1 egg yolk, beaten

Cut the carrot into strips about the size of your little finger. Cook the strips briefly in boiling salted water until just tender. At the same time, cook the fresh or frozen green beans until just tender. Drain and set aside.

Soak the bread crumbs in the milk. Add the meat, eggs, onion, and seasonings and mix well. Place one third of the meatloaf mixture in an 8½- by 4½-inch loaf pan. Make a layer of the reserved carrot strips. Put another third of the meat mixture on top; make a layer of green beans. Put the remaining meat mixture on top and press gently, pulling the meat away from the sides of the pan a little to firm the loaf.

Thaw the pastry shells, and set the dough in a rectangle, overlapping circles. Roll it into a rectangle, about 11 by 16 inches. Carefully take the meatloaf out of the pan and place it on the pastry. Pull the pastry up over the meat, overlapping and sealing the long edges. Place seam side down on a rimmed baking sheet. Brush with the beaten egg yolk, and cut 4 or 5 slashes in the top. Bake in a 375°F. oven for 1 hour. Cool on a rack.

Be prepared for the meat roll to lose some juice from the bottom while cooking, and to continue to drip a bit while cooling. Chill thoroughly. Slice it at home and wrap the slices individually. Makes 8 slices.

CHILLED CARROTS AMANDINE

Cook about 1 pound of carrots, washed, scraped, and cut in ¼-inch diagonal slices, in boiling salted water until tender. In a small skillet, cook ½ cup slivered blanched almonds in ¼ cup butter, stirring occassionally, for 3 to 4 minutes. Pour the almond butter over the drained carrots and chill. Decorate with minced parsley. Serves 4.

Packing Up

CHECK LIST B

COOLER

- ✓ meatloaf slices wrapped in plastic wrap
- ✓ artichokes wrapped in plastic wrap
- ✓ mayonnaise in a closed container
- ✓ carrots in a plastic container
- ✓ fruit in a rigid container
- ✓ wine

BASKET

- ✓ bread sticks
- ✓ coffee in a vacuum bottle
- ✓ plates and utensils
- ✓ ground cloth

At the picnic, give each person a slice or two of meatloaf and an artichoke. Pass the mayonnaise, the carrots, and the bread sticks, and enjoy your tasty treasure while you admire the incomparable view.

Mount Diablo State Park   5

Five miles east off Highway 680 from Danville on Diablo Road. Open 8:00 A.M. to one hour after sunset. Tables, barbecues, restrooms, water. Day use $2.

Though it is less than a mile high (3,859 feet) Mount Diablo sticks up from the surrounding low hills like a giant hand. It catches the flora and fauna that drift by, making it the northernmost and southernmost limit for many species such as the Coulter pine. Even without the marvelous views from the top, Mount Diablo would draw visitors for its diversity of wildlife, plant life, and geologic zones.

But it is the view that you will want to enjoy on your picnic. Do be sure to go clear to the top, either before or after the feast. On a very clear day, most often in late fall or winter, you may get a rare glimpse of Half Dome in Yosemite to the east, Mount Saint Helena to the north, the Farallones to the west, and, to the south, Mount Hamilton and the Santa Cruz Range.

When the valleys below are dampened in dreary fog, the peak is often enjoying clear sunlight, so try a winter or early spring picnic in a spot where you can bask in the sunshine, and barbecue a tempting feast as you watch the sun go down.

Several family picnic spots located along Summit Road—one appropriately called Sunset—offer views to the west. If you do stay for the sunset, remember that only the south gate through Danville will be open after 6:00 P.M., for one hour after sunset. Park regulations about fires change during the season. Wood fires are never allowed, but you may use charcoal or Presto logs unless fire danger is high.

As soon as you've chosen a spot, light the charcoal so the the coals will be ready. Open the wine, and enjoy a glass with the cheese puffs and vegetables while you wait for the fire.

Mount Diablo Leg of Lamb Barbecue

CHEESE PUFFS

RAW VEGETABLES WITH DILL DIP

BUTTERFLIED LEG OF LAMB

PILAF IN A POUCH

SLICED TOMATOES

FRENCH BREAD AND BUTTER

PEARS WITH COINTREAU

BEAUJOLAIS

COFFEE

CHEESE PUFFS

½ cup (1 stick) butter or margarine
1 cup all-purpose sifted flour
Dash of cayenne pepper

½ pound sharp cheese (Cheddar or New York)
1 tablespoon cold water

With a pastry cutter or knives cut the butter into the flour as you would for pie crust. Add the cayenne pepper. Grate the cheese and stir it in. Sprinkle with the cold water and mix with a fork until a dough forms. Shape into balls ½ inch in diameter. Bake on a cookie sheet at 375°F. for 10 minutes. Makes about 30.

BUTTERFLIED LEG OF LAMB

One 5-pound leg of lamb	1 teaspoon dried rosemary
4 tablespoons olive oil	1 teaspoon salt
2 cloves garlic, minced	1 teaspoon pepper

Split the leg of lamb and remove the bone. Combine the oil, garlic, and seasonings and marinate the meat in the seasoned oil at room temperature for 2–3 hours. Place the meat about 4 inches from the coals, and cook it for about 15 minutes on each side. Test by cutting a small slit in the thickest part. Serves 4 generously.

PILAF IN A POUCH

3 cups cooked rice	¼ cup chopped green onion
One-half 10-ounce package frozen green peas	1 teaspoon seasoned salt
	1 teaspoon dried basil
One-half 5-ounce can water chestnuts, drained and sliced	¼ cup butter, melted

Cut 4 pieces of aluminum foil into 18- by 12-inch rectangles. Press 1 piece of foil into a small bowl to make a pouch. Mix all the pilaf ingredients together and place one fourth in the pouch; seal securely. Repeat to make a total of 4 pouches. Place over the coals for 15 minutes. Fluff with a fork before serving. Makes 4 servings.

Packing Up

TO CHECK LIST C, ADD:

- ✔ extra plates for dessert
- ✔ a carving knife and fork

COOLER

- ✔ meat wrapped in plastic and placed in a container
- ✔ pilaf pouches
- ✔ tomatoes in a plastic container
- ✔ pears in Cointreau, in a plastic container
- ✔ butter in a self-sealing plastic bag
- ✔ raw prepared vegetables in a self-sealing plastic bag
- ✔ dip in a plastic container

BASKET

- French bread
- cheese puffs in a rigid container
- wine
- coffee in a vacuum bottle
- everything else on List B

SEPARATE SACK

- items on List C

Serve each person with the carved meat and one of the pilaf pouches. Pass the other things, and then settle back to wonderful food while you watch the sun go down.

Picnics for Ship Watchers

Three mini-parks, one in San Francisco and two in Oakland, offer unexcelled close-up views of ships, the workings of the ports, and the Bay itself. Because the largest one has only eight tables, and all three are fairly heavily used by local fishermen, I have given directions for finding them, but have not included them among the fifty picnic spots.

The largest, with a snack and bait concession and an observation tower, is Port View Park in the Seventh Street Marine Terminal in Oakland. From Highway 80, take the exit just before the toll plaza of the Bay Bridge and go southwest to Maritime Street. Follow it southwest to the end. Turn right on Seventh Street and follow the park signs.

Next largest, with three tables, is Middle Harbor Park, also in Oakland, just south of the U.S. Naval Supply Center. From Highway 17, take the Broadway exit and go west to Third Street. Follow Third Street northwest to Adeline and Middle Harbor Road. Go up over the overpass that crosses the tracks. Watch for the United States Lines on the left, and turn left here on Moorship Street. At the fork, turn left on Ferro and follow it to the park.

Smallest (we're down to one table now) is Agua Vista Park in San Francisco, south of Market in the Central Basin. Cross the Third Street Bridge and turn east on China Basin Street. Follow it south to between Sixteenth and Seventeenth. The park is on the left.

Benicia State Recreation Area   6

Take the Columbus Parkway exit east from Highway 780 1.5 miles northeast of Benicia. Tables, barbecues, restrooms, water. Entrance fee $2; coin-operated gate.

Any ship on its way from San Francisco Bay into the Delta and the deep-water channel to Sacramento or Stockton must pass through the Carquinez Strait, and you can have a front row seat for the show from the

Benicia State Recreation Area. On a clear winter or spring day, you'll see Mount Diablo across the water to the south, and through the strait, the Carquinez Bridge with San Pablo Bay beyond. Besides being a ship watchers' paradise, this water-oriented park is a good one for fishermen, bird-watchers, hikers, bicyclists, and joggers.

Have two dollars worth of change with you, as the park has an automatic gate. You can park just outside and walk the mile and a half along the road, which edges a salt marsh, out to Dillon Point and the picnic areas. It's an easy walk, and you're sure to see some interesting bird and plant life, but if it's at all hot, the walk can be tiring as there's no shade.

As you near the point, either on foot or by car, you'll see the parking area to your right. The nearby shady picnic area is on a pleasant grassy slope. More tables are located closer to the water as you continue on around the point, so check those out, too, and pick your spot before you unpack.

The Carquinez Strait, which you'll be looking across, is a 900-foot-deep submerged river canyon, formed as the Sacramento River eroded a channel to the sea through the rising coastal hills. When the ice melted after the last ice age, it raised the level of the sea and flooded the channel.

For one glorious year (1853) the city of Benicia was the capital of California, and on your way to or from the park you may want to visit the old State Capitol building, which is authentically furnished down to spittoons for the legislators. Camel barns used for holding military camels during the Civil War are among other interesting places to see in Benicia. If you find yourself there at mealtime, you can picnic on one of the rather cramped but well-shaded tables behind the old Capitol, or in the city park across from Solano Square. But ardent ship watchers will head for the State Recreation Area and its glorious views out across the northern reaches of the bay.

Benicia Fish Chowder Fare

ANTIPASTO ROLLS

FISH CHOWDER

CORNMEAL MUFFINS

SELECTION OF RAW VEGETABLES

GREEN HUNGARIAN WINE

APPLE PIE

COFFEE

ANTIPASTO ROLLS

¼ pound cheese, cubed
Small jar of pickled
 vegetables

¼ pound salami, sliced
Toothpicks

Bring all the ingredients to the picnic. Put some cheese and
pickled vegetables on a piece of salami, roll it, and hold with a
toothpick. These can be eaten with the fingers. Serves 4.

FISH CHOWDER

2 slices bacon, diced
1 onion, chopped
3 medium potatoes, peeled
 and cubed
1 stalk celery, chopped
1 green pepper, seeded and
 chopped
½ bottle (½ cup) clam juice
 or fish stock

1 pound firm white fish
 such as halibut, haddock,
 or snapper, cut into
 chunks
Salt to taste
½ teaspoon curry powder
3 cups milk

In a medium-sized saucepan, cook the bacon until crisp.
Remove, and pour off all but about 1 tablespoon of fat. Add
the onion and stir until just cooked. Add the potatoes and
other vegetables and clam juice or fish stock and simmer
about 15 minutes. Add the fish, the salt, and the curry
powder and simmer about 10 minutes more, or until fish is
firm. Add the milk and heat to just under boiling. Serves 4.

Packing Up

TO CHECK LIST B, ADD:

✔ bowls and large spoons
for the chowder
✔ server for the pie

Split and butter the muffins at home while they are still warm. Get the chowder and the coffee steaming hot, and put them in vacuum bottles.

COOLER

✔ raw vegetables in self-
sealing plastic bag
✔ wine

✔ antipasto ingredients in
self-sealing plastic bags

BASKET

✔ pie and muffins wrapped
in plastic wrap
✔ coffee in a vacuum bottle

✔ soup in a vacuum bottle
✔ all other equipment

At the picnic, pour everyone a glass of wine to enjoy with the antipasto rolls. Serve the chowder and pass the muffins. Relax and watch for you ship to come in through the strait.

Fort Point National Historic Site

7

From Highway 101 north, take the last exit before the toll plaza of the Golden Gate Bridge. To San Francisco, from Lincoln Boulevard, turn left onto Long Avenue. Proceed to Marine Drive and follow the signs left to the fort. Fort open 10 to 5, with tours hourly on weekends. Telephone (415) 556-1693. Restrooms, water. No tables, no barbecues. Free.

Not only do the city, the Bay, and Golden Gate Bridge look dramatic framed in the old gun ports of Fort Point, but the site, chosen to offer protection against an enemy invasion from the sea, commands a perfect view of all the ship traffic in and out of the harbour. It's hard to believe that only 130 years ago, this brick fort armed with muzzle-loading cannon was considered a worthwhile defense project. Obsolete almost before it was finished, the fort is now a National Historic Site, and rangers dressed in Civil War–era uniforms, authentic right down to the clumsy boots, will give you a tour.

You can peer out from the old gun ports for breathtaking peeks at the Bay, climb the stone spiral staircases, see the circular marks on the floor where the big cannons were pivoted, and visit the living quarters of the officers and enlisted men. A sunny day will give you the best viewing with the least chill factor at this windswept spot.

Leave the picnic in the car while you explore the fort, and when you've watched ship traffic to your heart's content, the grassy lawn near the parking lot makes a fine, sheltered spot to spread out a blanket or mat and enjoy your lunch. Planned in honor of the early Spanish settlers who constructed the first fort here, this picnic is easy to serve while sitting on the grass.

Fort Point Omelet-Sandwich Repast

TOMATOES STUFFED WITH RICE

SPANISH OMELET SANDWICHES

CORN CHIPS

FRESH FRUIT

GUAVA PASTE AND CREAM CHEESE

BLANC DE BLANCS

COFFEE

TOMATOES STUFFED WITH RICE

4 medium tomatoes
1 cup rice
¼ cup olive oil
2 tablespoons chopped
green onions

1 tablespoon fresh mint
leaves, chopped
1 teaspoon dried oregano
1 teaspoon salt
Dash of pepper

Slice the tops from the tomatoes, squeeze out the seeds, and scoop out the pulp with a spoon and chop. Cook the rice according to package directions. While still warm, add the remaining ingredients and the chopped tomato pulp.

Fill the tomatoes with the rice mixture and place in a shallow baking pan. Bake for 10 to 15 minutes at 400°F. Allow to cool and serve at room temperature. Makes 4.

SPANISH OMELET SANDWICHES

4 French rolls	1 clove garlic, minced
4 ounces each ham and cheese, sliced	1 medium tomato, peeled, seeded, and chopped
2 tablespoons oil	6 eggs
1 green pepper, seeded and chopped	½ teaspoon salt
1 medium onion, chopped	¼ teaspoon pepper

Cut the rolls in half and scoop out most of the soft insides. Top one half of each roll with a slice of ham, the other with a slice of cheese.

In a 10-inch frying pan, heat the oil and cook the vegetables, stirring, until soft. Lightly beat the eggs with a fork and add the seasonings. Pour the eggs in with the vegetables and cook, turning gently, until softly scrambled.

Spoon the cooked egg mixture onto the roll bottoms, add the tops, and wrap each sandwich in foil. Heat them in a 375°F. oven for 15 to 20 minutes. Wrap in layers of newspaper to transport hot to the picnic. Makes 4.

GUAVA PASTE AND CREAM CHEESE

Look for guava paste in the imported foods section of the supermarket. It comes in a loaf, like butter. Cut 2 slices per person, about 1 inch thick. Cut an equal number of slices of cream cheese and layer them with the slices of guava paste. Wrap each serving tightly in plastic wrap.

Packing Up

CHECK LIST B

NO COOLER NEEDED

BASKET

- ✓ tomatoes in a deep plastic container or bread pan, wrapped with foil, then newspaper
- ✓ sandwiches wrapped in plastic wrap
- ✓ corn chips
- ✓ fruit in a rigid container

- ✓ individual servings of guava paste and cream cheese
- ✓ wine
- ✓ coffee in a vacuum bottle
- ✓ plates and utensils
- ✓ ground cloth

When you've arranged yourself on the grass, give each person a sandwich and one of the tomatoes. Pass the corn chips and the wine. The soldiers probably didn't eat their omelets this way, but you'll find these delicious!

Coyote Point County Park 8

In Burlingame take the Peninsula Avenue exit east from Highway 101 and follow it to Coyote Point Drive. Open 8:00 A.M. to dark, daily. Telephone (415) 573-2529. Tables, barbecues, restrooms, water. Entry fee $2 on weekends. Coyote Point Museum open Tuesday through Friday 9 to 5; Saturday and Sunday 1 to 5. Telephone (415) 342-7755.

Coyote Point Park is a great place to watch the com-ings and goings of local navigators as they cruise near the marina, and to enjoy the wide view out over the Bay. The only possible drawback is that the many additional attractions here means that the park can get crowded, especially on summer weekends when swimmers come to the one spot on the Bay where the water is fairly warm.

Besides the beach and marina, a new museum re-creates all the surrounding ecological zones, from the tops of the hills down to the bayshore, with live animal exhibits and environmental displays. A golf course, a shooting range, a restaurant, a playground, and biking and hiking trails offer activities for everyone.

With this all-out barbecue picnic, you can come early and settle in, get your fire going, and take your time to enjoy all the park features. The picnic area is on the south side of the point near the marina, handy for boat watching; the beach is on the north side. Giant eucalyptuses shade the sturdy concrete tables and generously proportioned round barbecues. If you've chosen a cool day in order to have the place to yourself, bring something to sit on—those concrete benches get cold!

When you've chosen a table, get the fire going and enjoy some simple hors d'oeuvres while you wait for the coals to burn down.

Coyote Point Shish Kebob

SOFTENED CREAM CHEESE WITH WALNUTS

CRACKERS

OLIVES

SHISH KEBOB

BULGAR WHEAT SALAD (TABBOULEH)

FOIL-WRAPPED VEGETABLES

FRENCH BREAD

BAKLAVA

CABERNET SAUVIGNON OR BARBERA

COFFEE

SHISH KEBOB

1½ to 2 pounds lamb or beef, cubed
1 medium onion, chopped
1 clove garlic, crushed
1 teaspoon dried basil
½ teaspoon pepper
½ teaspoon dry mustard
1 tablespoon Worcestershire sauce

1 to 1½ cups red wine
Whole mushrooms
Pieces of onion, squash, and green pepper
Cherry tomatoes
Oil

Marinate the meat in a mixture of the onion, garlic, seasonings, and wine for 5 or 6 hours, or overnight. Remove from the marinade, and wipe off any bits that cling. On 5 skewers (1 for seconds) alternate the meat with the vegetables. Brush filled skewers with oil.

Place the skewers on the barbecue 6 to 8 inches from the coals. Cook about 15 minutes, turning frequently for even cooking. To serve, pull the foods on the skewer toward you, then push them off the skewer and onto a plate. Serves 4.

BULGAR WHEAT SALAD (TABBOULEH)

1 cup fine bulgar (cracked wheat)
6 green onions, chopped
½ cup fresh mint leaves, chopped
2 large bunches parsley leaves, chopped fine
4 tomatoes, chopped
½ cup olive oil
⅓ cup lemon juice
1 teaspoon salt
1 teaspoon pepper
4 large lettuce leaves (optional)

Soften the wheat by soaking it in water for 30 minutes. Drain and squeeze dry. Add all the remaining ingredients except the lettuce leaves and mix thoroughly. Chill. Serve on a large lettuce leaf if you wish. Serves 4.

FOIL-WRAPPED VEGETABLES

Make 4 individual packets of green beans wrapped in aluminum foil with about 1 tablespoon of chopped onion and a dash of salt added to each. Place them over the coals when you start the shish kebob.

Packing Up

TO CHECK LIST C, ADD:

✔ a small knife for spreading the cream cheese

COOLER

✔ shish kebobs (if skewers are too long to fit in the cooler, bring the ingredients and prepare them at the picnic)
✔ salad in a large plastic container
✔ foil-wrapped vegetables
✔ butter in a self-sealing plastic bag
✔ cream cheese in a small plastic container
✔ olives in a self-sealing plastic bag

BASKET

✔ crackers
✔ French bread
✔ baklava in a rigid container
✔ wine
✔ coffee in a vacuum bottle
✔ plates and utensils

SEPARATE CONTAINER

✔ charcoal, starter, matches

While you admire the boats tied up at the marina, the sailors will be admiring the aroma of your shish kebob. When it's ready, serve each person the contents of a skewer and one of the foil packets of green beans. Pass the salad and refill the wineglasses for a tasty, leisurely meal.

Angel Island State Park 9

Weekends and holidays throughout the year, and daily during summer, ferries go to the island from Pier 41, San Francisco (Harbor Carriers, telephone [415] 546-2815) from the Main Street Dock in Tiburon (Angel Island State Park Ferry, telephone [415] 435-2131) or in late spring and summer on weekends from the Berkeley Marina to East Garrison and back. Call ahead for schedules and fees. Tables, barbecues, restrooms, water. Ferry $2.50 adults, $1.25 children.

Angel Island is right in the thick of all the boat traffic that passes through the Bay. Large ships use the channel south of the island, while recreational boats use the north passage through Raccoon Strait. The excursion begins with a boat ride during which you'll probably see a number of fellow sailors in their boats enjoying a day on the Bay. At Ayala Cove, where the ferries land, you'll find the water dotted with private boats of all kinds and sizes.

The view depends on the side of the island you choose (Angel Island could also fit into "Picnics with a View"). To the northeast are the Richmond–San Rafael Bridge and the hills of Sonoma and Napa counties; to the west are Mount Tamalpais, Sausalito, and Tiburon; to the southwest are the Golden Gate and all the San Francisco waterfront; and to the east you'll see Richmond, Berkeley, Oakland—even Mount Diablo on a clear day.

Picnic tables with barbecues are located near Ayala Cove, but a short hike will take you to one of many spots where you can put down your ground cloth and enjoy boat watching away from the crowds. More tables are situated at the West Garrison, or on the top of Mount Livermore for the hardy. If you're in good condition, do climb up here for the best viewing of all.

For a less demanding hike that will give you ever-changing glimpses of the water and ship traffic below, take either the East Garrison or West Garrison trails for a twenty- to thirty-minute walk. These garrisons were established in the 1860s, and the buildings were in use until the 1940s. Another fifteen minutes' walk past West Garrison, a trail leads to Perles Beach where you'll find a picnic area with splendid views of San Francisco.

On the way to East Garrison, you'll pass Point Simpton, and North Garrison, which served as an immigration station, mostly for Asian immigrants. In 1941 it became a prisoner-of-war camp for German, Italian, and Japanese prisoners.

The food for this picnic is planned to go into day packs so you can hike a little or a lot to find the best place to eat while the ship traffic furrows the Bay below you.

Angel Island Wings and Nectar in a Knapsack

HEAVENLY CHICKEN WINGS

LEMON-PARSLEY BISCUITS

BROCCOLI WITH BACON AND WALNUTS

PARDUCCI VINTAGE CHABLIS OR
FETZER PREMIUM WHITE

ANGEL FOOD SQUARES WITH JAM

COFFEE

HEAVENLY CHICKEN WINGS

2 pounds chicken wings
½ teaspoon crushed dried
 red pepper
½ teaspoon black pepper-
 corns
1 teaspoon salt
⅛ teaspoon ground nutmeg
⅛ teaspoon ground cloves
⅛ teaspoon ground
 cinnamon
2 tablespoons oil

Trim the tips from the wings. In a small skillet, cook the pepper for 1 to 2 minutes. Crush in a mortar or with the flat blade of a knife. Stir in remaining seasonings.

Rub the chicken with the oil and place in a single layer on 1 or 2 baking sheets. Sprinkle with the seasoned salt, and bake at 400°F. for 45 minutes. Allow to cool before wrapping for the picnic. Serves 4.

LEMON-PARSLEY BISCUITS

Using biscuit mix or your favorite recipe, make biscuits, adding 2 teaspoons grated lemon peel to the dry ingredients. Add 2 tablespoons lemon juice and ¾ cup of chopped parsley with the liquid ingredients. Butter the biscuits while they are still warm, then wrap for the picnic.

BROCCOLI WITH BACON AND WALNUTS

½ pound broccoli
3 slices bacon, diced
3 tablespoons chopped
  green onions
½ cup coarsely chopped
  walnuts

Cook the broccoli in boiling water until just tender; drain. In a skillet, cook the bacon until crisp; transfer to a paper towel to drain. In the skillet, cook the onions in bacon fat for about 2 minutes. Add the nuts and cook, stirring, for about 5 minutes; drain. Combine with bacon. Sprinkle the broccoli with the bacon mixture, and when it's cool, package it in individual plastic sacks. Serves 4.

Packing Up

CHECK LIST B

You can delete the plates, knives, forks, and spoons unless you like to be neat. Let each person carry his own serving of chicken, biscuits, broccoli, and cake. Divide the wine, coffee vacuum bottle, water, and ground cloth among the day packs. When you've found the perfect spot to ship watch, each person can unpack his own wings, and you can serve the nectar to the vicarious voyagers.

Robert W. Crown Memorial State Beach

10

Take the Alameda exit from Highway 17 in Oakland, then go through the tube, which puts you on Webster Street in Alameda. Follow it to the end, then turn left along Central Avenue to the park. Telephone (415) 525-2233. Tables, barbecues, restrooms, water. Parking $1.25 on weekends.

The Oakland harbor and estuary are full of ships and boats, from sailboats with their colorful spinnakers to rusty tankers steaming slowly through the narrow channels. From Robert W. Crown Park on the Bay side of Alameda, you can see this traffic as boats enter the mouth of the Outer Harbor entrance to Oakland or the Inner Harbor on Alameda. You can keep an eye on the San Leandro Channel to the south as well.

Not only shipwatchers, but bird-watchers, hikers, swimmers, sunbathers, joggers, and bicyclists also find their particular territory. Tables and barbecues are scattered over the shady, grassy turf, and in sheltered spots closer to the water.

Once enjoyed by San Franciscans who crossed the Bay on a ferry to Neptune Beach for the Coney Island–style attractions, the shallow, relatively warm waters off Alameda have provided pleasant swimming for thousands of bathers. Over the years, the 2½-mile stretch of beach has been gradually losing a battle against eroding wind and water. Plans are in the works to bring in more sand, possibly from Angel Island, but in the meantime a minimal beach is still there, and the park can be enjoyed for many other features as well.

Because this beach is a popular place, our picnic is a marvelous breakfast, so we can get there early and find the best place to watch the ships sail by.

Robert Crown Trout Breakfast

MELON

BACON

CORN OYSTERS

CRISP-FRIED TROUT

MUFFINS OR SWEET ROLLS

COFFEE OR HOT CHOCOLATE

CORN OYSTERS

One 15-ounce can cream-
style corn
1 egg, beaten
1 cup saltine cracker
crumbs (about 28
crackers)

½ cup light cream
½ cup oil

At home, combine the corn, egg, and cracker crumbs. At the
picnic site, while half the bacon cooks, add the cream to the
batter and let it rest.

Put the bacon in a Pyrex dish near the coals to keep warm
while you cook the "oysters." Add more oil, if necessary.
Cook like pancakes, about 3 tablespoons of batter for each
one, browning on both sides. When done, put in the Pyrex
dish with the bacon, to keep hot while you cook the trout.
Serves 4.

CRISP-FRIED TROUT

4 large or 6 small trout
½ cup milk

½ to ¾ cup Bisquick
Bacon fat or oil

At home, behead the trout and remove the ventral fins. Dip
the fish in the milk, then in the Bisquick. Wrap it in plastic
wrap and keep it cold.

At the picnic, fry the remaining bacon first and use the
bacon fat to cook the trout. Fry the trout, not too fast, on both
sides until it is nicely browned and a fork pierces the back
easily. (If you don't wish to fry the fish in bacon fat, bring
some oil, but put a little piece of raw bacon in each body cavi-
ty to make the fish tasty and moist.) Serves 4.

Packing Up

TO CHECK LIST C, ADD:

- ✓ frying pan
- ✓ 2 extra plates
- ✓ steak knives for deboning fish

- ✓ mixing spoon
- ✓ spatula
- ✓ paper towels

COOLER

- ✓ trout wrapped in plastic wrap
- ✓ bacon wrapped in plastic wrap

- ✓ corn oyster batter in a plastic container
- ✓ cream in a carton
- ✓ melon

BASKET

- ✓ coffee or hot chocolate in a vacuum bottle
- ✓ muffins or rolls wrapped in plastic wrap

- ✓ container of oil
- ✓ plates and utensils from List C

EXTRA BASKET OR SACK

- ✓ charcoal (enough for a fire for 30 minutes)
- ✓ starter

- ✓ matches
- ✓ paper towels

At the picnic site, start the charcoal, mix the corn oyster batter, and enjoy the melon while the coals burn down a bit. Fry the bacon, reserving the fat. Keep it warm while you fry the oysters and then the trout. Serve the food with hot coffee from the vacuum bottle, and pour some more to go with the muffins or rolls. Meanwhile, keep an eye on the water for the passing parade of colorful ships and boats.

Picnics for Bird Watchers

Point Pinole Regional Shoreline Park

11

From Highway 80 just north of Richmond, take the Hilltop Drive exit west to San Pablo Avenue. Go north to Atlas Road, west to Giant Highway, and south for ¼ mile to the park entrance. Open 8:00 A.M. to dusk. Tables, barbecues, restrooms, water. Parking fee $1.25 on weekends.

When I ask my husband what he'd like to eat, one of his casual replies is, "Oh, just some hummingbirds' tongues poached in red wine." If you really wanted such a bizarre dish, Point Pinole would be the place to collect the hummingbirds. They swarm here by the hundreds when the eucalyptuses are in bloom, generally mid-March to April. Located under the Pacific Flyway, just south of Tubbs Island Refuge, this square-mile park offers an unusual variety of habitat—woods, meadow, freshwater and saltwater marshes, and beach —with a correspondingly rich mixture of bird life.

A meadowlark or red-shafted flicker may flash up as you make your way toward the shore. A red-tailed hawk or even a white-tailed kite may soar overhead. Once at the water you'll find grebes, loons, herons, or cormorants; while avocets, willets, plovers, and other shore birds inhabit the tidal flats. Gulls, of course, are wheeling everywhere.

As you walk through the park, you come upon the remains of a narrow-gauge railway and the abandoned concrete bunkers used by a series of gunpowder manufacturers from 1881 to 1960. Because of the formerly dangerous character of the place, the point remained isolated from the urban growth around it, becoming part of the park system in 1972.

The picnic area is at the end of Meadow Road. (On weekends a free shuttle bus will take you there.) Here you'll find a fine new fishing pier replacing the picturesque but unsafe old one, with tables that offer views in both directions. The marsh is to the east, the beach path to the south. Three and a half miles of San Francisco Bay shoreline are yours to explore.

When you're ready for some sustenance, pick your spot to picnic. This menu is a little easier to serve and eat at a table, but you could manage it seated on the ground. The soup can be served either hot or cold, depending on the weather. No hummingbirds' tongues here—this picnic consists of heartier fare.

Point Pinole Bird-Watchers' Potage

CREAM OF ZUCCHINI AND ALMOND SOUP

CORN PUDDING

CELERY ROOT, CARROT, AND WATERCRESS SALAD

FRESH FRUIT

CHENIN BLANC

TOFFEE SQUARES

COFFEE

CREAM OF ZUCCHINI AND ALMOND SOUP

1 medium onion, chopped
3 tablespoons butter
3 medium zucchini, sliced thin
½ cup slivered blanched almonds
4 cups chicken broth
½ cup ground blanched almonds
¾ cup heavy cream
1 tablespoon brown sugar
1 tablespoon Amaretto liqueur
¼ teaspoon ground cinnamon
¼ teaspoon ground nutmeg

In a kettle, cook the onion in the butter for about 5 minutes, or until soft. Add the zucchini and the slivered almonds and cook 5 more minutes. Add the chicken broth and simmer for 25 minutes. Add the ground almonds and simmer another 10 minutes. Stir in the remaining ingredients and cook, stirring, until heated through. Pour into a wide-mouthed vacuum bottle, or chill first if you want the soup cold. Makes 4 generous servings.

CORN PUDDING

3 tablespoons flour
1 teaspoon salt
¼ teaspoon paprika
¼ teaspoon dry mustard
Pinch of cayenne pepper
3 tablespoons butter
1 green pepper, seeded and
  chopped

½ onion, chopped
1 cup milk
2 cups fresh, frozen, or well-
  drained canned corn
  kernels
1 egg yolk, lightly beaten
⅔ cup buttered bread
  crumbs

Butter a 1½-quart baking dish. Mix the flour and seasonings together and set aside. Melt the butter in a skillet and cook the green pepper and onion until soft. Stir in the flour mixture and cook, stirring, for 2 or 3 minutes. Add the milk, stirring constantly, and bring to the boiling point. Stir in the corn and egg yolk.

Spoon into the battered baking dish and sprinkle with the crumbs. Bake for 25 minutes at 400°F. This can be well wrapped in newspaper to transport hot to the picnic or allowed to cool to room temperature. Serves 6.

TOFFEE SQUARES

These wonderful bars taste amazingly like English toffee!

1 cup butter, softened
1 cup packed brown sugar
1 egg yolk
1 teaspoon vanilla
2 cups all-purpose unsifted
  flour

¼ teaspoon salt
3 to 4 milk chocolate bars
  (about 4 ounces total)
½ cup chopped nuts

Cream the butter, sugar, egg yolk, and vanilla. Stir in the flour and salt. Pat into a rectangle on a 13- by 10-inch greased baking sheet, leaving 1 inch around the edge. Bake 20 minutes at 350°F.

Remove from the oven (the batter will be soft) and immediately place the separated squares of chocolate on top. Let stand until the chocolate softens, then spread evenly over the surface. Sprinkle with the nuts. Cut into small squares while warm. Makes 18.

Packing Up

TO CHECK LIST B, ADD:

✔ bowls or mugs for the
  soup
✔ soup spoons

NO COOLER NECESSARY

BASKET

- ✔ soup in a vacuum bottle
- ✔ salad, chilled, wrapped in newspaper
- ✔ corn pudding in its baking pan, wrapped in newspaper
- ✔ wine
- ✔ toffee squares wrapped in plastic wrap
- ✔ coffee in a vacuum bottle
- ✔ plates and utensils

When you've found the best spot to stop for lunch, serve the salad and corn pudding on plates. Put the soup in bowls, and with Peterson's field guide at the ready, enjoy all the gifts of nature around you.

Audubon Canyon Ranch   12

Three and one-fourth miles north of Stinson Beach on Highway 1. Open March 1 to July 4 from 10 to 4 on week-ends and holidays. Open to groups by appointment Tuesday through Friday. Telephone (415) 383-1644. Tables, rest-rooms, water. Free; donations welcome.

When the mother great blue heron returns to the nest in the redwood treetops in Audubon Canyon, the fledglings pounce on her and pull her head down, forcing her to give up the food she has brought back from nearby Bolinas Lagoon; the father heron gets the same treatment. Such behavior is not endearing, and eventually the parent birds just give up and don't return, leaving the babies to learn to fly and feed themselves on their own.

Looking down on this unexpectedly rough, noisy, lively scene from the observation post above the canyon is a fascinating experience. The canyon's shape allows an unequalled opportunity to look almost directly into the nests. The constant coming and going, squawking, and displaying of the huge birds makes an entertaining comedy. Egrets nest here, too, and when they fly, the spread of their white plumage against the dark green of the treetops is a breathtaking sight.

There's no reason why you couldn't carry your picnic up to the observation point, or beyond along one of the hiking trails such as the Bert C. Harwell Nature Trail, which makes a loop of just under a mile north of the canyon. You can pick up a trail map at the ranchhouse headquarters.

The picnic tables near the entrance to the ranch would be my choice of places to eat, but this menu can just as easily be stowed into day packs and carried to some other site.

Audubon Canyon Roast Pork Edibles

COLD ROAST LOIN OF PORK

FRENCH POTATO SALAD

ASPARAGUS WITH SESAME SEEDS

SALTED RUSKS

STRAWBERRIES WITH POWDERED SUGAR

GREY RIESLING OR CHENIN BLANC

COFFEE

COLD ROAST LOIN OF PORK

Serve a roast loin of pork (about 4 pounds) for dinner the night before, then bring the leftovers, sliced thin, to the picnic. Serve with a good French mustard.

FRENCH POTATO SALAD

4 or 5 potatoes
One 14½-ounce can beef
  broth
1 medium onion, chopped
8 cherry tomatoes, halved
One 4-ounce can artichoke
  hearts, drained and sliced

2 hard-cooked eggs, diced
1 tablespoon chopped
  parsley
Salt and pepper to taste

Boil the potatoes until tender. Drain, cool, peel, and slice. Marinate potato slices in the broth for an hour. Just before packing the salad, drain the potatoes and combine with the remaining ingredients. Serves 4 generously.

ASPARAGUS WITH SESAME SEEDS

1 pound asparagus	½ teaspoon soy sauce
2 tablespoons Oriental sesame oil	¼ teaspoon sugar
1 tablespoon lemon juice	2 tablespoons sesame seeds

Cut the asparagus on the diagonal into bite-sized pieces. Cook just until tender in boiling water, or steam. Combine the remaining ingredients with the asparagus; mix and chill. Serves 4.

SALTED RUSKS

Cut firm bread into thin, uniform slices, making at least 2 slices per person. Brush each slice with a little olive oil. Sprinkle sparingly with coarse salt and freshly ground pepper. Place the slices directly on the oven rack and bake at 200° to 225°F. until dry, about 1 hour. If you like garlic, rub the bread with a cut clove before drying. Cool the bread and pack it in a rigid, airtight container.

Packing Up

CHECK LIST B

COOLER

- ✔ sliced pork in a shallow rimmed dish
- ✔ potato salad in a plastic container
- ✔ asparagus in a plastic container
- ✔ strawberries in a self-sealing plastic bag
- ✔ wine

BASKET

- ✔ salted rusks in a self-sealing plastic bag
- ✔ powdered sugar in a small closed container
- ✔ mustard
- ✔ coffee in a vacuum bottle
- ✔ dishes and utensils

If you have a table, let people help themselves to the food while you pour the wine. If you've transferred the food to day packs and hiked somewhere, serve the plates and pass the wine. You'll see the great birds flapping their way to the lagoon for food while you enjoy yours with good companions.

James V. Fitzgerald Marine Reserve

13

Moss Beach, 4 miles north of Half Moon Bay off Highway 1.
Tables, restrooms. Free.

As its name implies, this low, rocky beach is a good place for tide pooling, and the visitor center can provide you with a booklet on marine life. Snorklers come in wet suits to pursue the elusive abalone well off shore. (No specimens may be removed from the reserve itself.) But the combination of freshwater and saltwater marshes also attracts many species of birds, some of them rare. You'll find long-necked cormorants, diving murres, willets, and brown pelicans. In the cypress trees above the beach you may even find a great horned owl.

At low tide, you can walk south all the way around Pillar Point to Princetown, about four miles, watching for bird life and marine life of all kinds as you go.

It is often foggy along this stretch of coast from June to September, so a good time to come is in either spring or fall when you may happen on a bright, clear day and when the bird migration will be at its height. Be ready for cool weather in either case, as when the fog is gone, it's generally because it has been blown away by the wind.

Fortunately, the picnic tables here are up near the parking lot and are quite well sheltered by the cypress trees that line the bluff above the beach. Bring your binoculars and bird book, of course, and wear nonslip shoes or boots for exploring the rocks.

Whether the wind has scoured the whole scene bright and sharp, or the softening fog is drifting in, this wild piece of coast makes adventurous exploring. Some hot food will almost surely be welcome here.

Marine Reserve Goulash Regalement

AUSTRIAN GOULASH

CUCUMBER SALAD

GARLIC BREAD

BURGUNDY OR BARBERA

CHOCOLATE POTS DE CREME

COFFEE

AUSTRIAN GOULASH

2 tablespoons lard or oil
2 large onions, chopped
1½ pounds lean beef in cubes
Salt to taste
1 tablespoon paprika
3 tablespoons tomato paste

½ teaspoon caraway seeds
½ cup red wine
One 14½-ounce can beef broth
3 potatoes, cooked and peeled

In a large saucepan or Dutch oven, melt the lard (or use oil) and gently cook the onions until limp. Add the beef, season with salt to taste, and add all the remaining ingredients except the potatoes. Cook slowly 2 hours. Add the cut-up potatoes and heat thoroughly. Carry the goulash to the picnic in a large, wide-mouthed vacuum bottle, or in a well-insulated or well wrapped heavy pot. Serves 4.

CUCUMBER SALAD

2 large cucumbers, peeled and thinly sliced
1 clove garlic, peeled and crushed

Salt
3 tablespoons vinegar
1 tablespoon sugar

Cover the cucumbers with water. Add the garlic and sprinkle well with salt. Stir. Let stand 1 hour. Drain. Discard the garlic and gently press water from the cucumbers. Add the remaining ingredients, stir gently, and chill. Carry the salad in a plastic container with a leakproof lid. Serves 4.

CHOCOLATE POTS DE CREME

This recipe is so easy that you won't want to tell anyone how you did it.

¾ cup milk
One 6-ounce package chocolate chips

1 egg
1 teaspoon vanilla
Pinch of salt

Heat the milk just to boiling. Put the remaining ingredients in a blender. Add the milk and blend at low speed for 1 minute. Pour into plastic glasses and chill. Makes 6 to 8 servings.

Packing Up

CHECK LIST B

COOLER

- ✔ cucumber salad in plastic container
- ✔ pots de crème in plastic glasses, covered with plastic wrap
- ✔ any utensils you have room for

BASKET

- ✔ well-wrapped goulash
- ✔ garlic bread
- ✔ wine
- ✔ coffee in a vacuum bottle
- ✔ plates and utensils

Dish out the hearty stew, and pass the cucumbers and garlic bread. Pour the wine and let the hot food restore your zest for more bird-watching and exploring.

Joseph D. Grant County Park   14

From San Jose take Alum Rock Road (Highway 130) east. Turn southeast on Hamilton Road. Open 8:00 A.M. until sunset. Telephone (408) 274-6121. Restrooms, water. No tables, no barbecues.

"Hairpin turn" is no mere figure of speech when you're talking about the road to the Joseph D. Grant Park, and especially if you decide to continue the ten more miles up to Lick Observatory on Mount Hamilton. It's a breathtaking ride with dramatic views, first out to the west over the Santa Clara basin, and then to the east through the hilly ranch land and increasingly steep slopes of the Diablo Range.

If you go on up to the observatory, you can visit the 120-inch telescope, one of the largest in the world. In the main observatory building is an exhibit of photos taken through the telescopes, and various astronomical instruments. The telescope is open from 10 to 5, and the photo exhibit from 1 to 5. Both are free. During the summer, the public may stargaze on Friday nights, but you must write (Visitors' Program; Lick Observatory; Mt. Hamilton, CA 95140) well in advance.

However fascinating the telescopes, our primary goal is bird life at Joseph D. Grant Park. Open to the public only since 1980, this park is a true wildlife sanctuary. The open ranch land, dotted with lakes and tree-filled creek beds, makes wonderful habitat for both resident and migratory birds. You'll probably be greeted near the visitors' center by a covey of quail nodding their way across the lawn with perfect poise and self-confidence. Everywhere you look, ground squirrels are scurrying from their burrows and then diving back to cover again. All this activity is not lost on the hawks, vultures, and buteos that circle in close over the hills. (Look alive!) Killdeer, owls, and Canada geese like the park, too.

The only designated picnic area with tables is for groups only, but you may picnic anywhere in the park. The rangers do request that you stay as near the trails as possible so as not to disturb the animals or plants. Among those whose peace is being preserved are some wild pigs, descendents from some escapees brought here from Europe to be hunted.

Stop at the visitors' center to pick up a trail map and check with the ranger as to where the best birding is on the day you arrive. With more than 9,000 acres to explore, you are sure to find a good birding-picnicking spot for this easy-to-carry repast.

Joseph D. Grant Quiche Comestibles

SPINACH QUICHE

STUFFED CELERY ROUNDS

MINIATURE MEATBALLS

FRESH FRUIT

CHABLIS

COOKIES

COFFEE

SPINACH QUICHE

4 eggs
2 cups light cream
½ teaspoon salt
⅛ teaspoon ground nutmeg
Pinch of cayenne pepper
½ cup grated Swiss cheese

1 cup cooked spinach,
  chopped and drained
2 tablespoons minced
  onion, sautéed in butter
One unbaked 9-inch pie
  shell

Combine the eggs, cream and seasonings in a bowl and beat
to mix thoroughly. Add the cheese, spinach, and onion. Be
sure the spinach is well drained.

Put this filling into the pie shell and bake for 15 minutes at
425°F., then at 350°F. for about 30 minutes more, or until a
knife inserted in center comes out clean. Cool. Cut in
serving wedges and wrap individually. Serves 4 to 6.

STUFFED CELERY ROUNDS

3 tablespoons butter,
  softened
3 tablespoons cream cheese

2 teaspoons anchovy paste
12 stalks celery

Cream all the ingredients, except celery, together thoroughly.
Then stuff the celery and press the stalks together to form
rounds. Wrap individual portions tightly in plastic wrap and
chill. Serves 4 to 6.

MINIATURE MEATBALLS

½ cup bread crumbs
¼ cup milk
1 onion, chopped
Oil or butter
2 pounds lean ground beef
½ cup minced parsley

2 mint leaves, chopped
2 egg yolks
2 cloves garlic, minced
2 teaspoons salt
¼ teaspoon pepper
4 tablespoons oil

Soak the bread crumbs in the milk and stir until blended. Sauté the onion in a little oil or butter until translucent. Add all the remaining ingredients except the oil.

Shape into bite-sized meatballs and brown in the oil in a skillet, slowly, until done inside, about 5 minutes. Drain and chill. Makes about 24, so put 6 apiece into 4 self-sealing plastic bags.

Packing Up

TO CHECK LIST A, ADD:

✓ wineglasses
✓ coffee cups

All the food can be eaten with the fingers from the plastic wrappings. If you prefer to be more elegant, use Check List B.

COOLER

✓ quiche portions wrapped individually
✓ celery wrapped in plastic wrap

✓ meatballs in self-sealing plastic bags
✓ fruit in a rigid container

BASKET

✓ cookies in a rigid container
✓ wine

✓ coffee in a vacuum bottle
✓ utensils if desired

At the picnic site, transfer the food and equipment to day packs and set off to find a portion of trees and sky filled with birds.

Sunol Regional Wilderness Park   15

From Highway 680 near Fremont, exit east on Calaveras Road just south of the town of Sunol. Continue five miles; turn left on Geary Road and proceed into the park. Open 8:00 A.M. to dusk. Telephone (415) 862-2244. Tables, barbecues, restrooms, water. Parking $1.25 on weekdays when a ranger is there to collect, $2.00 on weekends.

Sunol Regional Wilderness Park offers an outstanding variety of scenic attractions: a rocky canyon so lovely it's known as Little Yosemite; a creek dammed up for summertime swimming; open meadows and range-land; wildlife, including deer and cougars; fossil-embedded sandstone; massive basalt outcroppings for climbing; and, in the spring, carpets of wild flowers.

But the crowning glory is the birding. It's not uncommon to see from twenty to forty species in a single morning. Acorn woodpeckers, black phoebes, titmice, turkey vultures, and yellow-billed magpies are almost always at home, and sightings of golden eagles are made more often here than on Mount Diablo. It's hard to overstate how attractive this whole area is.

Naturalists often work with groups of school-children during the week, and lead programs for the public on weekends. Call ahead to see if you'd like to participate. At the headquarters you can pick up a map, a bird list, or borrow the wild-flower identi-fication list.

The wilderness character of the park is very seri-ously guarded. One ranger I spoke with even deplored the established picnic grounds along the creek as being an intrusion into the natural beauty, but I must con-fess I find them among the most delightful and appeal-ing places to open a picnic basket that I have found. Well separated from each other with off-the-road park-ing nooks, the attractive tables scattered along the broad creek cannot be resisted. But you shouldn't miss the beautiful hiking trails, either. If you walk along the Indian Joe Creek Trail, you can enjoy a creek and good birding, too. The 3-mile trail leads to cave rocks, and crosses the 1-mile nature loop trail. (Guides for this rent for 25¢ at the park office.) Canyon View Trail, 3.6 miles, leads to Little Yosemite with its weathered serpentine and sandstone outcrops. For an overview of the park, try at least part of the steep 2.8-mile climb up Flag Hill, 1,360 feet high. With binoculars ready, you're sure to find a variety of feathered friends on any of these excursions. After your hike, return to the creek to set out the sumptuous picnic that has been waiting in a cooler in the car. Lime water is served with this menu, as Sunol prohibits all alcoholic beverages, including wine and beer.

Sunol Golden Eagle Onion Tart Lunch

ONION TART

SLICED HAM

CHILLED BRUSSELS SPROUTS WITH CLOVES

PRETZEL STICKS

LIME WATER

ZUCCHINI BREAD

ONION TART

3 cups thinly sliced onions	¼ teaspoon pepper
3 tablespoons butter	⅛ teaspoon ground nutmeg
2 cups sour cream	⅛ teaspoon ground ginger
2 eggs, beaten	One 9-inch unbaked pie
1½ teaspoons salt	shell

Sauté the onions in the butter till soft and golden. Add all the remaining ingredients except the pie shell to the onions after mixing well.

Turn into the pie shell and bake at 450°F. for 10 minutes. Reduce heat to 350°F. and bake 30 to 40 minutes longer, or until a knife inserted in the center comes out clean. Serves 6.

CHILLED BRUSSELS SPROUTS WITH CLOVES

Cook about 16 Brussels sprouts in boiling water with 3 or 4 whole cloves added, until sprouts are just tender. Cool quickly in cold water. Dress lightly with melted butter and a dash of vinegar. Chill. Serves 4 to 6.

LIME WATER

This extremely refreshing drink has no calories and is delicious for any warm day. You use only the peels of the limes, so you can save the centers for other use.

5 limes
8 large mint leaves
2 quarts water

Peel the limes. Place the peels and mint leaves in the water. Cover. Refrigerate at least 24 hours. Remove peels before pouring into vacuum bottle. Makes 2 quarts.

Packing Up

TO CHECK LIST B, ADD:

- glasses for lime water rather than wine
- a server for the tart

COOLER

- onion tart in the baking pan, covered with plastic wrap
- sliced ham in a self-sealing plastic bag
- Brussels sprouts in a plastic container

BASKET

- pretzels
- zucchini bread, sliced and wrapped in plastic wrap
- vacuum bottle of lime water
- plates and utensils

Serve the onion tart, one or two slices of ham per person, and pass the Brussels sprouts and pretzels. Give everyone a generous glass of lime water and relax to the sound of bird song and the gentle lapping of the creek.

Picnics with Music

Concord Pavilion

16

Take the Ignacio Valley exit northeast from Highway 680 in Walnut Creek, and follow it about eight miles to the Pavilion. Prices of tickets vary with concert. Telephone (415) 798-3311 or 798-3316 for ticket information. Restrooms, water. No tables, no barbecues. Extra charge for parking. Free tram up hill.

An inviting bowl of grassy lawn surrounds the open-air stage at the Concord Pavilion, where picnicking before concerts is encouraged. You can stay on the grass during the show (tickets are cheapest this way) or move down to your reserved seat after the picnic. Old-timers like me fondly remember the beginnings of all this, when the Concord Jazz Festival took place in a small park on Concord Boulevard. We were all a little overwhelmed to have big-name stars willing to perform outdoors in such inauspicious surroundings. Big stars are still coming, but now they have a very sophisticated performing area. (Tours of the impressive backstage can be arranged by calling 798-3316.)

One other feature has remained constant from the old park setting to the new: it gets cold in Concord at night. Daytime temperatures in the eighties and nineties tempt early arrivers to dress lightly, but when night falls you'll need your down jacket (and mittens and hat), especially if you elect to sit on the grass for the concert.

One other problem at the Pavilion has to be overcome by the intrepid picnicker. The slope of the grassy area is excellent for providing a good view of the stage, but disastrous for attempting to serve food. Everything has a tendency to slide inexorably downhill. This can be averted, of course, with a little advance planning. It's fun to see the ingenious methods people use. Some friends of ours who are engineers brought cardboard boxes and cut them at an angle to the fit the slope, then laid a small board on top, and voila! a level serving table. You can try that if you need to serve a group, but it's really easiest to give each person a Bach's lunch and a pillow to set it against. That way everyone can fend for himself.

You can buy drinks at booths set up inside the grounds, but the Pavilion management does not permit cans or bottles to be brought in since such items can get away and wreak havoc rolling down the hill. Vacuum bottles are allowed, however, and one of the large pressure-dispensing types filled with hot coffee for that cold night I promised you will work well and be most welcome. Save some shoe boxes to pack the individual picnics in. They can be decorated with colorful paper if you enjoy doing that kind of thing. You may want to line the lid so it can serve as a tray.

Concord Pavilion Bach's Lunch

CHICKEN, CHEESE, AND CHILE ROLLS

DILLED CARROTS

PICKLE SPEARS

CELERY ROOT AND WATERCRESS SALAD

TORTILLA CHIPS

PETITS FOURS

CHICKEN, CHEESE, AND CHILE ROLLS

2 whole chicken breasts,
  halved
½ cup dry sherry
2½ cups chicken broth
4 tablespoons prepared
  mustard
½ teaspoon garlic salt
Good pinch each of dried
  sage, basil, and thyme

4 large slices jack cheese
4 strips canned peeled
  green chile
4 frozen puff-pastry shells
1 egg white, beaten
Sesame seeds

Poach the chicken breasts about 20 minutes in the sherry and broth. Let cool in the poaching liquid 30 minutes; remove, pull off the skin and remove the bones. Refrigerate.

Mix together the mustard and dry seasonings. Spread 1 tablespoon of the mixture over each piece of chicken, coating thoroughly. Wrap a slice of cheese, then a strip of chile around each piece.

Let the puff-pastry shells stand at room temperature 30 minutes. On a lightly floured board, roll each shell into an

8-inch circle. Set a piece of the wrapped chicken, seam side down, in the center of a pastry circle. Bring up the sides of the pastry to overlap in the center; moisten and pinch the dough to seal; repeat to make 4 bundles.

Place the bundles, seam sides down, on a large ungreased baking sheet. Brush with the egg white; sprinkle with the seeds. Chill 30 minutes. Bake at 425°F. for 30 minutes or until browned and crisp. Cool on a rack. Chill. Wrap individually and place in a box. Makes 4.

DILLED CARROTS

4 medium carrots, scraped and cut into strips	2 tablespoons butter ½ teaspoon dried dill weed

Cook the carrots in boiling water or steam until barely tender. Drain. Add the butter and dill. Chill. Pack in individual plastic sacks. Serves 4.

PETITS FOURS

Bake or buy your favorite loaf cake. Cut it into 3-inch squares (or other shapes if you feel inventive). Place cakes, 2 per person, on a rack and pour the following icing over them, coating tops and sides.

Icing

2 cups granulated sugar ⅛ teaspoon cream of tartar	1 cup water 1½ cups powdered sugar

Put the granulated sugar, cream of tartar, and water into a saucepan. Boil without stirring until it becomes a thin syrup, 226°F. on a candy thermometer.

Cool to slightly above lukewarm (100°F.) and gradually stir in the powdered sugar until the mixture is just thick enough to coat a spoon. Pour over the cake while warm. You can color the icing with food coloring, or add 3 ounces unsweetened chocolate, melted. Use proportionately less chocolate if you're adding it only to part of the frosting.

Packing Up

INTO EACH OF 4 SHOE BOXES, PUT:

- ✔ 1 chicken roll, wrapped
- ✔ 1 serving of carrots in a plastic sack
- ✔ 1 serving of tortilla chips
- ✔ 2 individually wrapped petits fours
- ✔ a portion of the salad in a small container with a lid
- ✔ a napkin and fork

BASKET

✓ coffee	✓ cups
✓ cream and sugar	✓ ground cloth

As you watch the golden hills of Contra Costa County fade into the dusk, pour everyone another cup of hot coffee, put on your jacket, and prepare to listen to the concert in casual comfort.

Joaquin Miller Regional Park and Woodminster Amphitheater

17

From the Warren Freeway (Highway 13) in Oakland, take the Lincoln Avenue exit east. This is Joaquin Miller Boulevard. Take the Robinson Drive entrance left into the park. Telephone (415) 273-3181. Woodminster Amphitheater: (415) 531-9597. Tables, restrooms, water.

One of a string of parks that sits atop the Oakland hills, Joaquin Miller could easily qualify as a "Picnic with a View." The Oakland Estuary and Lake Merritt are laid out below as neatly as on a map, and the Bay sparkles beyond with San Francisco and the Golden Gate in the distance. To the north is the Berkeley campanile peeking up above the trees. Because the Woodminster Amphitheater's summer productions offer an extra incentive to picnic here, I've put this picnic in the music category so you can look forward to a performance after an elegant outdoor supper.

Joaquin Miller's poetry is not much read anymore, but the other legacy he left us is enjoyed by thousands of people every day. He reforested the logged-off Oakland hills with 75,000 trees, returning the area to much of its original beauty. In 1919 his land, which he called "The Hights," was acquired by the Oakland

Park Department from his widow and their daughter, Juanita, who continued to live on the property for many years.

While Miller lived there, he constructed a series of monuments: a miniature castle to honor the Brownings, a battlementlike structure for John C. Fremont, a pyramid for Moses. Near this Moses monument is a lovely picnic area with shady tables and a drinking fountain. From the Robinson Drive entrance, go past the ranger station toward Robin's Roost and Lookout Point. (Thousands of robins do roost here during the spring and fall migrations.) Make the circle back toward the entrance on the lower road, and you'll see several picnic tables, each in a lovely spot for watching the sunset over the Bay.

Joaquin Miller Poached Salmon Provender

THIN-SLICED RYE BREAD WITH CREAM CHEESE AND RADISHES

POACHED SALMON WITH DILL SAUCE

TYROPITA (FILO WITH CHEESE)

CUCUMBER MOUSSE

BLANC DE BLANCS OR GREY RIESLING

FRESH RIPE PEACHES & CHOCOLATES

COFFEE

POACHED SALMON WITH DILL SAUCE

One 2-pound chunk
    salmon, or 2 pounds
    salmon steaks
1 onion, chopped
1 carrot, chopped
1 stalk celery, chopped
2 tablespoons butter
2 tablespoons chopped
    parsley

1 whole clove
1 bay leaf
2 teaspoons salt
4 peppercorns
¼ cup dry white wine
Lettuce leaves (optional)
Dill Sauce, following

Wrap the salmon in cheesecloth, if you like, to make it easier to remove from the poaching liquid. In a large pan sauté the vegetables in the butter until soft. Add the seasonings and the wine, then water to cover. Cover and simmer 5 minutes. Uncover and add the salmon. Simmer, covered, 10 minutes or until the fish flakes easily.

Chill in the stock, then remove and wrap for the picnic. For a pretty presentation, wrap first in lettuce leaves. Serve topped with the following sauce. Serves 4.

Dill Sauce

To 1 cup of homemade mayonnaise, add ¼ cup sour cream, 2 teaspoons lemon juice, 1 tablespoon chopped fresh chives, and 1 tablespoon chopped dill weed, fresh if possible. Carry to the picnic in a separate container.

TYROPITA (FILO WITH CHEESE)

¼ pound feta cheese,
  crumbled
⅔ cup cottage cheese
1 egg, beaten

3 leaves filo dough
¼ cup butter, melted
1 tablespoon chopped
  parsley

Mix the cheeses and add the egg. Following the directions on the package for handling, cut the filo dough into 3-inch strips and brush with the melted butter, making 3 layers.

Place 1 large teaspoon of the cheese mixture on 1 end of the dough and fold the corner over to make a triangle. Continue folding from side to side in the form of a triangle until end of strip. Refrigerate for 30 minutes before baking.

Place on buttered baking sheet, brush butter on top, and bake in a 350°F. oven about 15 minutes. Sprinkle with the parsley. Cool and wrap for picnic. Serves 4.

CUCUMBER MOUSSE

4 medium cucumbers
1 cup boiling water
2 tablespoons lemon juice
2 teaspoons Worcestershire
  sauce
1 teaspoon salt

½ teaspoon white pepper
1 cup mayonnaise
2 envelopes (2 tablespoons)
  unflavored gelatin
¼ cup water
1 cup heavy cream

Peel the cucumbers, cut them in half, and remove the seeds. Blanch cucumbers about 5 minutes in the boiling water with the lemon juice. Drain, put in a blender, and blend to pulp.

Cool the pulp and add the seasonings and mayonnaise. Dissolve the gelatin in the ¼ cup water. Add to the cucumber. Whip the cream until stiff and fold into the cucumber mixture. Pour into a wet 4-cup mold and chill.

Unmold. Wash mold and oil lightly. Replace the mousse in the mold for transporting to the picnic. Serves 4 to 6.

Packing Up

TO CHECK LIST B, ADD:

- ✓ server for the mousse
- ✓ butter knives for cream cheese

COOLER

- ✓ salmon in its serving container
- ✓ dill sauce in a plastic container
- ✓ cucumber mousse in the oiled mold
- ✓ tyropita in a serving dish, wrapped in plastic wrap
- ✓ fresh peaches in a rigid container

- ✓ cream cheese in a small plastic container
- ✓ radishes in self-sealing plastic bag
- ✓ rye bread wrapped in plastic
- ✓ chocolates individually wrapped
- ✓ wine

BASKET

- ✓ plates and utensils
- ✓ the optional tablecloth (this picnic deserves one!)

When you've chosen your table, set out the bread, cream cheese, and radishes and let people help themselves. Give them a glass of wine, then finish setting the table and putting out the food. The view, the sunset, the tasty food should put you in a perfect mood for the outdoor music to follow. Don't forget the tickets.

Mount Tamalpais Mountain Theatre   **18**

Mount Tamalpais State Park; 801 Panoramic Highway; Mill Valley, CA 94941. Telephone (415) 388-2070. From Highway 1, take Panoramic Highway north to Bootjack Area. Open 8:00 A.M. to half an hour after sunset. Tables, restrooms, barbecues, water. Mountain Play Association;

Marin Box Office, Civic Center; San Rafael, CA 94903. Telephone (415) 472-3500. Free shuttle buses every 20 minutes from 11:00 A.M. to 1:00 P.M. from Mill Valley Middle School, Mill Valley Bus Depot, and Highway 1 at Tam Junction.

Mount Tamalpais, with its stunning views of the entire Bay Area and its fascinating diversity of natural environments, is a place that people want to visit again and again. A man-made attraction that fits in beautifully with the surrounding natural terrain is the Mountain Theatre, with its impressive scenic back-drop two thousand feet above sea level. The amphi-theater is in a natural bowl with massive tiers of serpentine rock that I'm sure the ancient Greeks would have enjoyed.

Performances by the Theatre Artists of Marin are usually scheduled on Sunday afternoons during May and June, and they provide an extra incentive to picnic on the mountain. Tickets are reasonably priced and can be ordered by calling the number above, or by visiting a local ticket agent. You can bring the picnic up to the theater and spread you edibles out on the sun-soaked stones, or walk a little way up the Rock Springs Trail and find a spot to your liking.

Bootjack Picnic Area on Panoramic Drive, the only fully equipped one in the park, is only seven-tenths of a mile away, a pleasant walk through shady groves of eucalyptuses and redwoods; so you may want to drive there, have a picnic, and then walk to the theater. (Parking in the area of the theater is extremely limited.)

If the day is foggy, you'll have to bundle up, but re-member that when the rest of the Bay Area is swathed in dampness, Mount Tam is often riding high in the sunshine, so bring a sun hat and suntan lotion for the performance—and maybe some cushions for those stone benches. This picnic will go in your day pack in case you decide to take the free shuttle bus or hike a bit to a secluded picnic site of your choosing.

Mount Tam Portable Taco Picnic

TACOS

BEAN SALAD

FRESH FRUIT

MEXICAN BEER

DESSERT CHIMICHANGAS

COFFEE & WATER

TACOS

1 pound lean ground beef
1 onion, chopped
4 ounces (½ can) tomato
  sauce
⅓ to ½ cup refried beans
2 teaspoons chili powder
½ teaspoon dried oregano
¼ teaspoon ground cumin
¼ teaspoon pepper

1 tablespoon fresh cilantro,
  chopped (if you like it)
¼ cup oil
1 dozen small corn or
  wheat tortillas
2 tomatoes, chopped
2 onions, chopped
1½ cups chopped lettuce
1 cup grated cheese

Brown the meat in a large frying pan; drain fat. Add the onion
and sauté until limp. Stir in the tomato sauce, beans, and seasonings and simmer, uncovered, until hot.

In another large frying pan, heat about ¼ inch oil. To allow
the tortilla to fold without breaking, hold it by the edges with
both hands and let a center strip cook in the hot oil until
lightly softened. Remove the tortilla, fill it, and fold it over.
Fry the filled tortillas on both sides until crisp. Drain on
paper towels.

Carry the tomatoes, onions, lettuce, and cheese to the
picnic in separate self-sealing plastic bags and spoon into the
tacos just before eating. Makes 12 (3 per serving).

BEAN SALAD

1 cup canned red kidney
  beans
1 cup cooked green beans
3 green onions, finely
  chopped

¼ cup French dressing
  (oil and vinegar type)

Drain the kidney beans, rinse, and dry. Cut the green beans
into bite-sized pieces. Mix the beans with the onions and
dressing. Refrigerate for at least 2 hours to let the flavors
blend. Makes 4 servings.

DESSERT CHIMICHANGAS

1 dozen small flour
  tortillas
3 cups chopped walnuts
½ cup butter, softened
½ cup honey
1½ teaspoons ground
  cinnamon

1½ teaspoons ground
  allspice
1 egg white, beaten
  with 2 teaspoons water
Oil for frying
Powdered sugar

Heat the tortillas, wrapped in aluminum foil, in a warm oven until they are pliable.

To make the filling, combine the walnuts, butter, honey, and spices. Spoon about ¼ cup of the filling in a strip at one side of the tortilla. Brush the remaining surface of the tortilla with the egg white and fold the tortilla around the filling, tucking in the sides so it forms a rectangle. Moisten the ends with the egg white mixture and lay seam side down; repeat to fill all tortillas. Let tortillas stand several minutes to allow the egg white to dry and seal.

To cook, put 1½ inches of oil in a large pan and deep fry at about 375°F., turning until golden brown. Drain on paper towels. Sprinkle with powdered sugar. When cool, pack in a rigid container. Makes 12 (3 per serving).

Packing Up

COOLER

- tacos individually wrapped in plastic wrap, then in heavy paper
- taco garnishes in plastic bags
- bean salad in individual serving cups
- fresh fruit
- beer

BASKET, OR ALREADY IN DAY PACKS

- chimichangas, individually wrapped
- napkins
- plates, if you like
- forks
- spoons
- vacuum bottle of coffee
- bottle of water
- cups
- powdered cream
- sugar

When you get to the parking lot, transfer the picnic to day packs and enjoy your stroll to the picnic ground and amphitheater. If you're carrying a cushion, put that in first, then put the tacos and chimichangas on top so they won't get squashed. To serve, pass around the taco garnishes so everyone can be on his own to enjoy this portable western meal.

Villa Montalvo   19

Montalvo Center for the Arts; P.O. Box 158; Montalvo Road; Saratoga, CA 95070. Telephone (408) 867-3421. From Highway 9 one-half mile south of Saratoga, take Montalvo Road west. Grounds open daily 8 to 5. Villa open 1 to 4 except Monday. For schedule and prices of performances, call number above. Restrooms, water. No tables, no barbecues. Fee 50¢ on weekends.

In 1912, James D. Phelan, who had been mayor of San Francisco and U.S. senator from California, built a summer home in the foothills of the Santa Cruz mountains. Phelan was a millionaire and a lover of the arts. (One of the great disappointments of his life was that during a thirteen-year feud with John Muir over the Hetch Hetchy resevoir, he was accused of being insensitive to beauty.) When he died, this architectural gem, surrounded by 175 acres of formal gardens and wooded trails, was willed to the public as a center for creative activities in the arts. Monthly exhibitions are mounted in the three galleries on the main floor of the villa, and concerts, plays, and lectures are given in the Carriage House Theatre. A few lucky artists and musicians with approved creative projects live in furnished apartments on the grounds.

A picnic before a performance at the Villa Montalvo can take you back to those turn-of-the-century times when leisurely afternoons were spent strolling through gardens, watching for birds, and quietly enjoying the loveliness of nature, tamed your pleasure. You can spread out a blanket on the huge sweep of lawn that leads up to the pillared veranda, or perhaps seek some shade under one of the rare specimens of trees. The formal beauty of the setting seems to call for rather elegant fare, so here is a Mediterranean menu, designed for easy serving.

Villa Montalvo Pasta Primavera

SHRIMP-STUFFED TOMATOES

PASTA PRIMAVERA

BREAD STICKS

FRESH FRUIT

CHARDONNAY OR SAUVIGNON BLANC

ITALIAN TORTE

COFFEE

SHRIMP-STUFFED TOMATOES

4 good-sized tomatoes	1 tablespoon chopped
Salt	parsley
½ pound cooked small	Dressing, following
shrimp	4 sprigs parsley
1 cup frozen artichoke	
hearts, cooked	

Peel the tomatoes. (Blanch in boiling water a minute to make the skins easy to remove.) Cut the tops off and remove the seeds and pulp. (The end of a spoon works well.) Lightly salt the insides.

In a bowl, combine the shrimp with the vegetables. Mix lightly with the following dressing. Fill the tomatoes with the shrimp mixture, topping each with a sprig of parsley. Wrap individually in plastic wrap. Chill thoroughly. Serves 4.

Dressing

½ cup mayonnaise	1 clove garlic, minced
¼ cup Dijon mustard	½ teaspoon pepper

Stir all the ingredients together until well blended.

PASTA PRIMAVERA

If the thought of cold pasta leaves you feeling likewise, try this. It will convert you!

¾ pound of pasta,	2 tablespoons oil
such as spirals or	1 clove garlic, minced
shells	¼ cup olive oil
3 cups 1-inch pieces	Salt
assorted vegetables, such	Freshly ground pepper
as asparagus, green	½ cup fresh basil leaves,
beans, zucchini	chopped
4 medium tomatoes	¼ cup chopped walnuts

Cook the pasta in boiling water until just tender. Cook the vegetables quickly in boiling water just until crisp. Peel, seed, and chop the tomatoes.

In a frying pan, heat the 2 tablespoons oil with the minced garlic. Add the tomatoes and cook gently for 3 minutes. Season with salt and freshly ground pepper. While the pasta is still lukewarm, toss it with the olive oil. In a large bowl, stir together the pasta, tomatoes, and vegetables. Add the basil and nuts. Chill. Serves 4 generously.

ITALIAN TORTE

This recipe calls for a can of almond paste, which is expensive stuff, but there are so few other ingredients that the total cost is not prohibitive.

One 8-ounce can almond paste	¼ teaspoon salt
3 tablespoons flour	2 eggs
½ teaspoon baking powder	6 tablespoons dry-roasted sunflower seeds

Crumble the almond paste into a large bowl with your fingers or a fork. With a mixer, blend in all the remaining ingredients except for the sunflower seeds.

Spread the batter evenly in a 9-inch removable-bottomed cake pan that has been buttered and floured. Sprinkle the sunflower seeds over the top. Bake at 325°F. for 40 minutes. Cool 10 minutes and remove outer rim of pan. This is a torte, not a cake, and will stay quite flat. Be prepared for pointed questions about what happened to your cake, until people taste it. It will carry well wrapped in plastic wrap. Makes 8 servings.

Packing Up

CHECK LIST B

You may want to bring real plates and glasses for this picnic.

COOLER

- ✔ stuffed tomatoes, in deep container such as a bread pan
- ✔ pasta in a bowl or plastic container
- ✔ fruit in rigid container
- ✔ wine

BASKET

- bread sticks
- torte cut into servings, wrapped in plastic wrap
- coffee in a vacuum bottle
- dishes and utensils
- ground cloth or tablecloth

When you've had a chance to unwind and enjoy the beauty of the setting, serve each picnicker a stuffed tomato and some pasta. Pass the bread sticks and pour the wine. Then drink a toast to Mr. Phelan and his love of art, music, and good living.

Robert Mondavi Winery 20

West side of Highway 29 just north of Oakville; 781 Saint Helena Highway. Concerts on Sunday at 7. No picnicking at other times. For tickets call (707) 963-JASS. Restrooms, water.

Concerts in the vineyards are one of the delights unique to California. Few things are so pleasant as consuming a sybaritic picnic in the golden afternoon and then settling down for a treat to the ears. The Robert Mondavi Winery jazz concerts usually begin in late June and continue on through July. This series is popular, so you will need to write or phone well in advance for tickets.

Unfortunately, the granddaddy of these performances at the vineyards—the Charles Krug August Moon concerts—has been discontinued, the sponsor of the programs having withdrawn financial support due to increased costs. Geyser Peak Winery, which had sponsored a delightful theater and music series, has had similar problems. Paul Masson Winery continues its popular presentations, but picnicking is not permitted at these concerts, though there is champagne tasting at intermission.

At Robert Mondavi, picnicking is situated on the grassy area in the courtyard, and an extremely enthusiastic audience has usually assembled long before the performance begins, so plan to be early to set up your portable all-out feast.

Not only is the architecture of this winery extremely appealing, with its bold arches and covered walkways, the wine produced here is excellent. Both the Red and White Table wines have taken an upturn recently, again being blended with Napa grapes and aged in oak. (*New West* magazine, May 1981, says, "No funny stuff, just a slam dunk.") The White Table Wine is a fine choice for a reasonably priced bottle of very good wine. If you want to spend more—ten to thirteen dollars—try one of the Sauvignon Blancs, which would be excellent with this picnic. (Mondavi Cabernets are extremely good, and there is no reason why you could not drink a bottle of red wine with this menu, though my choice would be Sauvignon Blanc.)

Mondavi Chicken and Pesto Mélange

CHICKEN AND PEA SALAD WITH PESTO

VEGETABLE-STUFFED SHELLS

SMOKED MOZZARELLA WITH OLIVE OIL AND PEPPER

BAGUETTE

SAUVIGNON BLANC

FRESH FRUIT WITH SOUR CREAM AND
BROWN SUGAR

COFFEE

CHICKEN AND PEA SALAD WITH PESTO

Salt and pepper
3 pounds chicken, or 2
    pounds chicken breasts
2 cups chicken broth
Pesto Sauce, following

4 lettuce leaves
2 cups shelled fresh raw
    green peas
Pine nuts

Lightly salt and pepper the chicken. Simmer, covered, in the chicken broth for 20 to 25 minutes. Let cool in the broth, then remove, skin, bone, and cut meat into 1½-inch chunks. Mix with the pesto sauce, following. Cover and chill.

Serve the salad on a lettuce leaf with the fresh peas sprinkled on and around it. Sprinkle with a few pine nuts. Serves 4.

Pesto Sauce

2 cups loosely packed
    fresh basil leaves
2 cloves garlic
¼ cup grated Parmesan
    cheese

6 tablespoons olive oil
⅓ cup pine nuts or dry
    roasted sunflower seeds

In a blender or food processor, blend all the ingredients until smooth.

VEGETABLE-STUFFED SHELLS

16 jumbo pasta shells
1 cup chopped fresh
    broccoli
1 cup shredded raw zucchini

½ cup chopped mushrooms
¼ cup sliced green onions
Sauce, following

Cook the shells according to package directions until just tender. Drain, cover with cold water, and drain again. Mix the vegetables with half the following sauce, then use them to stuff the shells. Chill. Top with extra sauce before serving. Serves 4.

Sauce

1 cup heavy cream
2 tablespoons lemon juice
2 tablespoons chopped
    fresh dill

Salt to taste

Blend all the ingredients until slightly thickened.

SMOKED MOZZARELLA WITH OIL AND PEPPER

Lightly coat about 8 slices of smoked mozzarella cheese with olive oil. Sprinkle with freshly ground pepper. Serves 4.

Packing Up

CHECK LIST B

COOLER

- ✔ chicken salad with pesto (lettuce leaves in a plastic sack, raw peas and nuts or seeds in separate sacks)
- ✔ stuffed pasta shells in a deep container
- ✔ separate container of extra dill sauce
- ✔ mozzarella cheese arranged on a rimmed platter, tightly sealed with plastic wrap
- ✔ container of fresh fruit with sour cream and brown sugar

BASKET

- coffee in a vacuum bottle
- dishes, glasses, and utensils
- baguette
- wine, if you are not going to buy it at the winery

When your blanket and tablecloth are spread out and everyone has a glass of wine, serve each person some of the salad on a lettuce leaf with the raw peas around the edge. Serve the pasta shells with some additional sauce. Pass the smoked cheese and the sliced baguette and wait confidently for sighs of contentment.

Picnics
with
History

John Muir Home National Historic Site

21

Exit Alhambra Valley Road from Highway 4 in Martinez. Open daily 8:30 to 4:30. Telephone (415) 228-8860. Tables, restrooms, water. Entrance 50¢.

Enter the John Muir house through the visitors' cen-ter, where you can see a short and informative film on the famous conservationist's life before taking the self-guided tour of the house. Charmingly furnished, details of the house decoration include clothes hanging in the closets and a state of homey disorder in Muir's study, with books and papers everywhere, so that you feel the great naturalist might suddenly appear and begin writing again. Even the attic with its cuppola has old trunks and cast-off furniture.

The house was originally built by his father-in-law, but Muir himself farmed the 2,600-acre ranch very successfully, producing hundreds of tons of cherries, grapes, and other fruits. He made enough money this way to support his family and still have time for exploring and writing. As a picnicker, you'll be interested to know that you're invited to help yourself to any fruit that is ripe at the time of your visit. Depending on the season, that could be peaches, cherries, pomegranates, quinces, oranges, apricots, pears, grapes, figs, apples, or lemons!

After your visit to the main house, retrieve the picnic from the car and stroll through the orchard to the adjacent Martinez adobe. Built by Don Vicente Martinez in 1849, this house is unfurnished, but you can go in and admire the construction.

Two picnic tables are set behind the adobe under a shady canopy. If they are in use you can spread out a ground cloth on the nearby grassy area, but the rangers request that you do not picnic elsewhere on the grounds.

On my last visit to the John Muir home, I overheard a ranger telling a group of schoolchildren that Muir

82 | 50 GRAND PICNICS

survived on dry bread balls, sugar, and tea while he was out in the wilderness, but here in civilized territory, you can indulge yourselves in a Scots-style lunch in honor of Muir's heritage. In order to encourage his children to be on time for meals, Muir used to tell them a serialized story at dinner. Maybe someone in your picnic party can oblige with a tale!

John Muir Home Ploughman's Lunch

CRUSTY WHOLE-WHEAT BREAD

ENGLISH CHEDDAR OR FARMHOUSE CHEESE

SCOTCH EGGS

PICKLED BEETS & FRESH VEGETABLES

FRESH FRUIT

BEER OR ALE

OATMEAL COOKIES

TEA, HOT OR ICED

SCOTCH EGGS

6 hard-cooked eggs, peeled
¾ pound bulk pork sausage
2 eggs, beaten

¾ cup bread crumbs
3 tablespoons butter

Cover each hard-cooked egg with a layer of the raw sausage meat, about ¼ inch thick. Dip the sausage-covered eggs into the beaten eggs, then dip in the bread crumbs to coat.

Fry the eggs slowly in the butter, turning continually until the sausage is cooked on all sides, about 10 minutes. This recipe obviously makes 6 servings, or 4 servings with 2 extra to be split for second helpings.

OATMEAL COOKIES

These cookies can be kept in a tin or frozen.

½ cup butter, softened
½ cup solid shortening
1 cup sugar
1 teaspoon vinegar
¾ cup milk

1 teaspoon baking soda
2 eggs
1 cup sifted all-purpose flour
2 cups regular oatmeal
1 cup raisins

Cream the butter, shortening, and sugar. Mix the vinegar into the milk, then stir in the soda. Add the eggs, flour, and milk alternately to the batter, about one third at a time. Add the oatmeal and raisins. (If you mix a little flour into the raisins they won't stick together in the batter.)

Place tablespoonfuls of the batter on a lightly greased cookie sheet and bake at 375°F. about 12 minutes. Makes about 4 to 5 dozen.

Packing Up

CHECK LIST B

You won't need the spoons, wineglasses, or corkscrew.

COOLER

- ✓ cheese wrapped in plastic wrap
- ✓ Scotch eggs individually wrapped
- ✓ pickled beets, sliced and placed in a container with a tight lid
- ✓ fresh vegetables cut into bite-sized pieces, in a plastic container
- ✓ fresh fruit in a rigid container, to supplement what you can pick
- ✓ beer or ale

BASKET

- ✓ bread
- ✓ oatmeal cookies
- ✓ tea in a vacuum bottle
- ✓ plates and utensils
- ✓ ground cloth

I imagine that John Muir didn't have very many pub lunches like this one, but he certainly knew something about ploughing, so perhaps a ploughman's lunch on his land would meet with his approval. When you've settled at a table or on the grass, give everyone something to drink. Cut the bread and cheese and pass it with the Scotch eggs and other foods. Don't forget to have someone start an exciting story to be continued on your next visit.

Black Diamond Mines Regional Preserve

22

Take the Somersville Road exit south from Highway 4 in Antioch. Open 8:00 A.M. to dusk. Telephone (415) 757-2620.

Tables, barbecues, restrooms, water. Parking fee $1.25. Mine tour $1.00 for adults, 50¢ for children.

A tour inside an abandoned mine, a visit to a pioneer cemetery, and a look at an authentic archeological dig are all good reasons to bring a picnic to Black Diamond. A visit here takes you back a century as you explore what was once California's largest coal mining development: "black diamonds" were dug here for almost a hundred years. Children love this park, and the rangers do a splendid job of explaining things. With its 3,343 acres of grassy hills and scattered oaks, Black Diamond is a prime spot for spring wild flowers, too, so late March or April is a good time to come. Phone ahead to see what activities are planned and to arrange to go into one of the silica mines in the company of a ranger. Everybody wears a hard hat with a lamp and imaginations can run wild.

From the park entrance you can see cypress trees on the top of a hill that once separated two old towns. The trees point heavenward and mark Rose Hill Cemetery, where you can examine the headstones, many of them with the Welsh names of miners and their families. (Never go into any of the mine shafts without a ranger; some mines are extremely dangerous because of accumulated carbon dioxide.)

Nothing else remains of the six mining towns that were here, but if you've always thought it would be fascinating to hunt for archeological artifacts, you can see a real dig on the site of Somersville, where students from the University of California at Berkeley are conducting a systematic exploration.

A walk through the mine, a climb up to the cemetery, or a hike around the Chaparral Loop can work up an appetite, so here's a hearty meal. Picnic tables are located near the entrance to the mine and near the Somersville site.

Black Diamond Miners' Stew

MINER'S STEW

GREEN SALAD

FRENCH BREAD & BUTTER

FRESH FRUIT AND CHEESE

LEMON BARS

BURGUNDY OR ZINFANDEL

COFFEE

MINERS' STEW

1½ pounds beef chuck, cut into cubes
2 tablespoons oil
1 cup hot water
1 teaspoon lemon juice
1 teaspoon Worcestershire sauce
1 clove garlic
1 medium onion, sliced
1 bay leaf
2 teaspoons salt
½ teaspoon pepper
Dash of whole cloves
1 teaspoon sugar
6 carrots, scraped and cut up
4 medium potatoes, peeled and quartered
1 to 2 tablespoons flour mixed with ¼ cup cold water (optional)

In a Dutch oven, brown the meat on all sides in the hot oil. Add all the remaining ingredients except the carrots, potatoes, and flour-water mixture. Simmer covered 2 hours, stirring occasionally. Add the carrots and potatoes and continue cooking 20 to 30 minutes. Thicken the liquid, if necessary, with the flour dissolved in water.

To transport to the picnic, get the pot full of stew very hot. Wrap it in a towel, then in several layers of newspaper, or put it in an insulated container. Serves 4.

LEMON BARS

¼ cup (½ stick) butter or margarine
1½ cups finely crushed Ritz-type crackers
½ cup all-purpose unsifted flour
½ cup sugar
Lemon Filling, following

Cut the butter into the remaining ingredients. Spread half the cracker mix in a 13- by 9-inch pan. Spread the lemon filling over it, then top with the remaining cracker mixture, patting it down lightly. Bake at 375°F. for 30 minutes. Makes 18 bars.

Lemon Filling

3 eggs
¼ cup butter or margarine

1 cup sugar
1½ tablespoons lemon juice

Beat the eggs in a saucepan. Add the remaining ingredients and cook and stir over medium heat until thick. Cool before using.

Packing Up

CHECK LIST B

COOLER

- ✓ green salad, dressing separate (if you bring the salad greens in a large plastic sack, you can pour the dressing in and toss the salad in the plastic sack)
- ✓ fresh fruit in a rigid container
- ✓ cheese wrapped in plastic wrap

BASKET

- ✓ stew well-wrapped to stay warm
- ✓ French bread, already buttered, wrapped in plastic wrap
- ✓ lemon squares wrapped in parcels of 2
- ✓ wine
- ✓ coffee in a vacuum bottle
- ✓ plates and utensils

After the table is secured and the plates and utensils are laid out, serve everyone some hot stew and salad. Pass the buttered bread and pour the wine. It hasn't been very many generations since mining families must have admired the same view while they ate their dinners, too. Good appetite!

Petaluma Adobe State Historical Park   23

From Highway 116, one mile east of Petaluma, take Casa Grande Road 2.5 miles north. Open 10–5. Telephone (707) 996-1744. Tables, restrooms, water. Admission 50¢. Ticket good for all features of Sonoma State Historic Park.

Just a glance at the place names on a map of California reminds us that Spanish-speaking people settled the state first. One of the most powerful and respected of those early Californians was General Mariano Guadalupe Vallejo: officer in charge of the Presidio in San Francisco, political leader during the formation of the state, and master of a 100-square-mile agricultural empire near the present-day city of Petaluma.

The land grant given to Vallejo in 1834, in the hope that he could help discourage the Russians from further settlements in California, reached from San Pablo Bay in the south to Glen Ellen in the north, and from Petaluma Creek in the west to Sonoma Creek in the east. The *casa grande* served as more than a home; it was the administrative center for all the activities on the ranch.

A self-guided tour of the house shows you authentic furniture, a kitchen with a beehive-shaped oven, looms for weaving wool grown on the ranch, and other tools and equipment of rancho life.

The state has been working on an ambitious restoration of the ranch since 1951, and details such as hides—the main cash crop of the ranch—hanging on the fences to dry have been carefully attended to. As you drink in the peace of the tranquil countryside that still surrounds the adobe, it's easy to imagine yourself back in what we like to think of as simpler times.

The house, a beautiful example of Monterey-style architecture, sits on high ground with sweeping views over the hills and valleys, still peacefully rural. Some tables are located near the house, and others are near the creek you cross on the way from the parking lot. The rancheros might not have eaten this exact meal, but the ingredients were all at hand on the ranch.

Petaluma Adobe Comida Campestre

BEEF TONGUE OR COLD BEEF VINAIGRETTE

RANCH-STYLE BEANS

TORTILLAS

FRESH RAW VEGETABLES

CALIFORNIA FRUIT SALAD

ZINFANDEL OR BURGUNDY

COFFEE

BEEF TONGUE OR COLD BEEF VINAIGRETTE

On the California ranchos, cattle were raised for their hides;
the meat tended to be tough and stringy, so the tongue was
the prized cut. If you don't care for it (and I must confess that I
don't!) substitute any cold sliced meat with the vinaigrette
sauce.

1 fresh beef tongue, or 1
   pound sliced cooked beef
   brisket
1 carrot, cut into pieces
2 stalks celery, cut into
   pieces

Parsley
1 bay leaf
Salt and pepper to taste
Sauce Vinaigrette, following

If using tongue, cook until tender in boiling water to which
the remaining ingredients have been added. This will take
from 2 to 3½ hours.

Allow tongue to cool in the broth, then remove the skin
and slice the meat thin. Arrange overlapping slices of meat in
a Pyrex dish, and pour the following sauce vinaigrette over
it. Marinate the tongue or other meat in the sauce several
hours or overnight in the refrigerator. Serves 4.

Sauce Vinaigrette

1 cup oil
½ cup wine vinegar
1 tablespoon chopped
   parsley
2 tablespoons chopped
   fresh chives
2 tablespoons chopped
   onion

1 tablespoon chopped green
   pepper
1 teaspoon paprika
1 teaspoon prepared
   mustard
3 hard-cooked eggs, chopped

Mix all ingredients together.

CALIFORNIA FRUIT SALAD

Use at least four kinds of fruit in season. A basic combination is peaches, apricots, plums, and strawberries. Tropical fruits such as kiwis, papayas, mangos, and bananas add a pleasant touch. Bring the following dressing separately. Carry the fruit, splashed with juice from 1 lemon, in a large plastic sack and, at the picnic, add the dressing to the sack and gently toss it to coat.

Fruit Dressing

½ teaspoon salt
¼ teaspoon white pepper
1 tablespoon grenadine syrup
½ teaspoon grated orange rind

½ teaspoon grated lemon rind
½ cup good cider or wine vinegar
¾ cup oil

Add the seasonings to the vinegar and mix well with a fork. Add the the oil gradually, stirring constantly. The dressing may also be made in a bottle and shaken.

Packing Up

CHECK LIST B

COOLER

- chilled meat in the sauce in a deep container
- fresh raw vegetables in a self-sealing plastic bag
- fruit salad in a self-sealing plastic bag
- fruit dressing in a plastic container

BASKET

- ranch-style beans, heated, wrapped in newspaper
- tortillas, wrapped in aluminum foil packets of

4, then heated and wrapped in newspaper
- wine
- coffee in a vacuum bottle
- plates and utensils

At the picnic table of your choice, serve everyone some beans, then pass the meat and the tortillas. Serve one packet at a time to keep the others warm. Serve the fruit salad later, with coffee. The rancheros would have been drinking wine made from Mission grapes, but you will have to settle for Zinfandel or Burgundy. The aura of early California will surely hover about you as you have your *comida campestre* on this peaceful site.

China Camp State Park   24

From Highway 101 north of San Rafael, exit east on North San Pedro Road. Telephone (415) 456-0766. Tables, barbecues, restrooms, water. Day use $2.

When the gold mines played out and the transconti-nental railroad was completed, the Chinese workers who had helped to build the West needed new employment. China Camp was one of the thirty fishing villages along the Bay in which they settled in the 1860s. Chinese shrimp fishermen took advantage of the sunny hillsides to dry their catch of bay shrimp, which was then exported to China, until this practice was banned in 1905.

All that's left of the village of nearly five hundred people that once stood here is a few ramshackle buildings along the water. This is the center of activity in the park, and you can rent a boat or buy a shrimp cocktail or a beer. On a sunny Sunday, the small beach by the pier is full of happy sunbathers.

Besides this historical area, China Camp offers the visitor 1,500 acres of the most natural watershed remaining along the shore of San Francisco Bay. Intertidal, salt marsh, meadow, and oak habitats provide shelter for a variety of wildlife, water birds, and shore birds, and at the fishing access anglers can sometimes find striped bass, flounder, silver and rubberlip perch, and even an occasional sturgeon.

You can picnic on the beach, but if you like a little more privacy, Weber and Buckeye points, on the way to the historical center, have picnic tables with barbecues and offer lovely views out over the water past Pratt's Island, which seems to have a particularly Chinese look about it. Maybe I'm just suggestible!

For an interesting prepicnic walk, take the trail to Jake's Island, which you'll spot just inside the perimeter of the park. The trail starts at a triangular metal gate on the south side of the hill, goes along a broad lane at the foot of Chicken Coop Hill, and continues out to the former island. The land has gradually filled in so that you can walk dry-shod except during the very highest tides. Wild iris is plentiful here in the spring, and you can climb to the top of the island for more views out over the water.

If you prefer an inland ridge hike, take the Back Ranch Trail, which leads south from the road just inside the park and circles around to join the Miwok Trail farther down the road.

After exploring the park, you can come back to Weber or Buckeye Point for a shrimp barbecue. Some bay shrimp is still taken from these waters, but as you can't count on being lucky enough to find some on the day you arrive, you'll need to bring some shrimp along.

China Camp Shrimp Barbecue Special

RICE WITH EGGPLANT

BARBECUED MARINATED SHRIMP

FRESH VEGETABLES WITH SOUR CREAM DIP

FRENCH BREAD

FRESH FRUIT IN KIRSCH

CHEESES

DRY CHAMPAGNE

COFFEE

RICE WITH EGGPLANT

1 eggplant, about 1 pound
2 tablespoons butter or margarine
½ cup finely chopped onion
1 teaspoon minced garlic
½ teaspoon freshly ground pepper
½ cup crushed canned tomatoes

1 bay leaf
½ teaspoon dried thyme
⅛ teaspoon crushed dried red pepper
½ cup rice
1 cup chicken broth

Trim and peel the eggplant, and cut it into ½-inch cubes. You will have about 3½ cups. Heat the butter in a saucepan and add the onion and garlic. Cook, stirring, until the onion is wilted. Add the eggplant and the ground pepper. Stir. Add the remaining ingredients, except rice and broth. Cook, stirring occasionally, for about 3 minutes. Add the rice and broth. Cover. Bring to the boil and let simmer for 20 minutes. Make 4 pouches from heavy-duty aluminum foil and divide the rice among the pouches. Seal securely by twisting the tops. At the picnic, reheat by placing over the grill for 15 minutes. Serves 4.

BARBECUED MARINATED SHRIMP

1 to 1½ pounds raw shrimp
   (approximately 20 to 30
   per pound)
1 tablespoon crushed dried
   red pepper
2 cloves garlic, minced
¾ cup oil
½ teaspoon salt

Shell and devein the shrimp. Wash under cold running water and pat dry. Combine the remaining ingredients in a blender and blend until well mixed. Marinate the shrimp at least 2 hours in the refrigerator in this mixture.

Put the shrimp on small wooden skewers, running the skewers through the middle of the shrimp, not lengthwise. A skewer will hold 5 or 6 shrimp. Put them in a closed container to transport to the picnic. At the picnic site, place the skewers on the grill and cook 1 to 2 minutes on each side. Serves 4.

Packing Up

CHECK LIST C

Bring small bowls for dessert instead of plates. Bring plenty of napkins.

COOLER

- ✓ skewered shrimp in a container covered with plastic wrap
- ✓ rice with eggplant in foil packets
- ✓ fresh vegetables and dip in containers with lids
- ✓ fresh fruit in kirsch in a covered container
- ✓ cheese wrapped in plastic wrap
- ✓ champagne

BASKET

- ✓ French bread
- ✓ coffee in a vacuum bottle
- ✓ plates and utensils

EXTRA SACK

✔ charcoal and other items
from Check List C

When the charcoal is started and the coals are burning down, you can set out the rest of the picnic. Open the champagne and start on the vegetables while you wait. The shrimp will take only 2 to 4 minutes, so start the rice first. It can stay warm while you do the shrimp. Open the rice pouches and stir the contents to fluff a little. To deskewer the shrimp, pull them toward you with a fork, then push them off the skewer. They won't be quite the same as the tiny bay shrimp that the Chinese caught, but they will be delicious indeed!

Robert Louis Stevenson State Park   25

Seven miles north of Calistoga on Highway 29. Tables. No barbecues, no restrooms, no water. Free. Silverado Museum, 1490 Library Lane, St. Helena. In downtown Saint Helena, go east on Adams Street to the end, then left on Library Lane. Telephone (707) 963-3757. Open noon to 4 daily except Monday. Free.

If your childhood memories include snatches of rhymes from *A Child's Garden of Verses*, or you still suppress a shiver at the thought of Blind Pew and John Silver in *Treasure Island*, then a picnic on the site where Robert Louis Stevenson spent his honeymoon has to be an exciting proposition. The famous writer, with his bride, Fanny Osbourne; her son by a former marriage; and a setter-spaniel named Chuchu (whom Stevenson describes as being the least suited of the four for the rough life), camped out for the summer of 1880 in an abandoned bunkhouse near the played-out Silverado mine in Napa County. Stevenson wrote a book—*The Silverado Squatters*—about their adventures, and eventually the state park surrounding the old mine site was named in his honor.

Before you reach the park, stop in Saint Helena for a preliminary briefing at the Silverado Museum. Please note that the museum has moved from its former downtown location in the Hatchery Building (this now houses the Belle Helene Restaurant, but no cheating—we're here for a picnic!) to its own wing in the new Saint Helena Library building.

Displays of Stevenson memorabilia from all over the world fill the charming red-carpeted rooms. The volunteers who staff this small gem of a museum will gladly give you details on Stevenson's life and career.

When you're ready to go on to the park, continue north on Highway 29 for seven miles and watch for the park entrance on your left. There are picnic tables near the parking lot, but the trail up to the cabin site is so pleasant and the picnic we've planned is so light that you can easily carry your supplies up to the very spot where the bunkhouse stood. Pick up a trail guide at the entrance so you won't miss anything along the way. Ambitious hikers can go on five or more miles to the top of Mount Saint Helena, which at 4,343 feet is higher than either Mount Tamalpais or Mount Diablo.

Stevenson described his Napa home in *The Silverado Squatters:* "A rough smack of resin was in the air and a crystal mountain purity. It came pouring over these green slopes by the oceanful. The woods sang aloud, and gave largely of their healthful breath. Gladness seemed to inhabit these upper zones, and we had left indifference behind us in the valley." He would be glad to know that it hasn't changed.

Silverado Squatters' Tasty Meat Roll Nurture

STUFFED FRENCH ROLLS

SPINACH TARTS

STUFFED PEARS, STUFFED AVOCADOS

FAVORITE COOKIES OR BARS

BURGUNDY OR ZINFANDEL

COFFEE

STUFFED FRENCH ROLLS

4 French rolls
3 tablespoons butter
1 clove garlic
3 tablespoons mayonnaise
1 pound cooked meat, sliced
(leftover roast is great)

2 dill pickles, sliced
lengthwise
12 pitted green ripe olives,
sliced

Hollow out the rolls by slicing them in half and pulling out some of the soft insides. Melt the butter and squeeze in the garlic with a garlic press. Brush the insides of the rolls with the garlic butter, then spread lightly with the mayonnaise. Layer in the centers the meat, pickles, and olives. Put the halves together and press down firmly. Wrap tightly with plastic wrap. Serves 4.

SPINACH TARTS

1 package (6) frozen puff-
pastry shells
One 10-ounce package
frozen chopped spinach
2 eggs, beaten
¼ cup milk

¼ teaspoon dried dill weed
¼ teaspoon garlic salt
2 tablespoons minced onion
1 ¾ cups shredded Swiss or
jack cheese

Prepare the patty shells as directed on the package, but bake only until puffed, about 30 minutes. Remove the center caps from the shells and scoop out any soft dough in the centers. Thaw the spinach and squeeze out all moisture. Mix the spinach with the eggs, milk, seasonings, and cheese.

Pack the spinach mixture gently into the shells and bake at 350°F. about 15 minutes. Cool to room temperature and wrap in plastic wrap. Makes 6 tarts.

STUFFED PEARS

2 pears
1 tablespoon lemon juice

2 finger-sized pieces cream
cheese

Cut the pears in half and core. Sprinkle the cut sides with the lemon juice. Put the cream cheese in the centers and reassemble. Wrap with plastic wrap. Refrigerate until time to leave. Serves 4.

STUFFED AVOCADOS

2 avocados
1 teaspoon lemon juice
4 tablespoons mayonnaise

1 teaspoon dry mustard
Dash of bitters

Peel, halve, and seed the avocados. Rinse in cold water and sprinkle with the lemon juice to prevent darkening. Combine the mayonnaise with the seasonings and fill the avocado centers. Put the halves together and wrap tightly with plastic wrap. Refrigerate until time to leave. Serves 4.

Packing Up

CHECK LIST B

Delete the silverware. Bring along day packs to transfer the picnic supplies to before starting up the trail.

COOLER

- ✔ sandwiches individually wrapped
- ✔ stuffed pears wrapped in plastic wrap
- ✔ stuffed avocados wrapped in plastic wrap
- ✔ spinach tarts wrapped in plastic wrap

BASKET

- ✔ cookies in a self-sealing plastic bag
- ✔ wine
- ✔ coffee in a vacuum bottle
- ✔ plates, glasses, and utensils

When you reach the cabin site, you'll find it marked with a memorial plaque in the shape of an open book. Spread out your ground cloth and hand around the food, all of which can be eaten with the fingers. The clear, pure air that restored Stevenson's health will make you feel wonderful, too.

Picnics in the Wine Country

Sonoma Plaza

26

Highway 12 leads directly to Sonoma Plaza. Tables, barbe-cues, restrooms, water. Sonoma State Historic Park is on the north side of the plaza. Historic sites open daily 10 to 5. Telephone (707) 996-1744. Fee of 50¢ allows you to enter all exhibits.

In the wine country of the Sonoma and Napa valleys, many a would-be picnicker, bread, cheese, wine, and fruit in hand, has gazed longingly at the lovely shady grounds of Beringer Brothers in Saint Helena, or the oak-studded lawns of Domaine Chandon at Yount-ville, only to realize that picnicking is not permitted. It's not that winery owners are inhospitable (think of all the free wine they dispense!), it's that they can't afford the staff necessary to keep a picnic ground orderly or to handle the crowds that would be attrac-ted. Just be grateful for the wine tasting and don't despair. Picnickers *are* welcome in many places in the wine country.

The Sonoma Plaza, for example, is a picnicker's dream. Originally, I hadn't intended to include it because I thought everyone would know about it any-way, but it is such an attractive city park—large, with deeply shaded lawns beneath venerable trees, and, best of all, ringed with specialty shops that can sell you all your picnic supplies—that I couldn't leave it out.

For example, French bread from the Sonoma Bakery at 470 First Street East is better than other bread; why is a mystery. You can also buy an elegant dessert here. At the northeast end of the block across from the Mis-sion is the Sonoma Creamery, which has sandwiches, deli supplies, drinks, and so on. On the north side of the square is the Sonoma Cheese Factory, which sells, besides cheese, sandwiches and other supplies. You can eat your picnic on the little terrace here, but I prefer the more tranquil square. The state park build-ings, including Mission San Francisco Solano de Sonoma and the Sonoma Barracks, are also on this side. Just a half mile east on Spain Street is Lachryma Montis, General Vallejo's home, which also has some picnic tables in a shaded arbor up behind the house. (I'll bet you thought I'd never get to the following picnic menu, which must be everybody's all-time favorite!)

Sonoma Sandwich Lunch

CRUSTY FRENCH BREAD

YOUR CHOICE OF MEATS AND CHEESES

PICKLED MUSHROOMS

DELI SALAD

SONOMA BAKERY DESSERT

A WINE YOU'VE TASTED

Packing Up

CHECK LIST A

TO BUY ON THE WAY

✔ all menu items

Buena Vista Winery (The Haraszthy Cellars) 27

From the southeast corner of the Sonoma Plaza, go east on East Napa Street, cross the railroad tracks, and go northeast on Old Winery Road to the end. Open daily 10 to 6. Telephone (707) 938-8504. Tables, restrooms, water.

Not only is Buena Vista a fascinating winery to visit— it is the original winery founded by the legendary Count Haraszthy in 1857—but it also has a charming picnic area. Tables are placed on a slope beside the winery, and also next to a bubbling stream in front of the old stone building.

The vineyards you see as you drive in are part of the original holdings where Count Haraszthy planted the first European varieties of wine grapes brought to California. The count, a Hungarian, had searched all over the United States for a suitable wine-growing area, and found it in the Sonoma Valley. Exhibits inside the winery, which is now a state historical site, give you details of this fascinating story. As you survey the peaceful vineyards and the vine-covered winery, it's easy to believe that not much has changed since that time.

Vineyards seem to have an aristocratic quality not usually associated with other kinds of farms. Maybe the end product lends a certain panache to the enterprise, or maybe it's just the close-in surrounding hills providing a beautiful contrast with the orderly rows of grapes. Whatever the reason, the following picnic is a rather elegant spread to match the high standards of cuisine often encountered in this region.

If you prefer, you can easily stop and buy supplies in Sonoma (see Picnic 26).

Buena Vista Pâté Lunch

TOMATO BOUILLON

LEEK PÂTÉ

BAGUETTE

LAYERED SALAD

BUENA VISTA WHITE WINE OF YOUR CHOICE

PEARS WITH BLUE CHEESE

COFFEE

TOMATO BOUILLON

One 10¾ ounce can tomato soup	¼ cup chopped green pepper
1 soup can cold water	¼ cup chopped green onion
¼ cup chopped cucumber	

Mix the soup with the cold water and chill. Bring the chopped vegetables in a separate plastic sack. At the picnic, pour the chilled soup into mugs and add the vegetables. Serves 4.

LEEK PÂTÉ

4 large potatoes
4 leeks
½ cup butter, melted
½ cup plain yogurt
1 package (1 tablespoon) unflavored gelatin dissolved in ¼ cup white wine

3 green onions with tops, sliced
Salt and white pepper to taste

Boil the potatoes about 25 minutes or until tender. Peel and press through a ricer. Trim the leeks and cook 2 of them whole in boiling water to cover until soft. (A large frying pan works well.) Cool and separate into leaves. Line the bottom and sides of a lightly oiled 8½- by 4½- by 2½-inch loaf pan with the leaves, saving some for the top.

Roughly chop the remaining leeks and cook in boiling water until tender, about 20 to 25 minutes. Drain, and then add them to the potatoes. Stir in the butter, yogurt, gelatin mixture, and green onions. Season with salt and pepper to taste and pack firmly into the lined pan. Top with the remaining leek leaves. Cover and chill for at least 5 hours. At the picnic, unmold and slice into thick slices with a very sharp knife. Serves 6.

LAYERED SALAD

⅓ head iceberg lettuce, shredded
½ large red onion, minced
1 green pepper, seeded and coarsely chopped
2 stalks celery, sliced
¾ cup shelled fresh green peas, blanched briefly in boiling water
1 cup mayonnaise (home-made if possible)

¼ cup freshly grated Parmesan cheese
1 tomato, peeled and seeded
¼ cup lemon juice
¼ cup chopped watercress
4 strips of bacon, cooked and crumbled
12 pitted black olives, quartered
1 hard-cooked egg, sliced

The day before the picnic, layer the lettuce, onion, pepper, celery, and peas in a large plastic container. Spread the mayonnaise evenly over the top and sprinkle the Parmesan over the mayonnaise. Cover and refrigerate overnight. Cut the tomato into strips and marinate the strips overnight in the lemon juice.

Before leaving for the picnic, sprinkle first the watercress, then the bacon, on the salad. Drain the tomato strips and arrange them on top. Add the olives, then the egg. At the picnic, serve by digging down through the layers. Serves 4 to 6.

Packing Up

TO CHECK LIST B, ADD:

- bowls or mugs for the soup

COOLER

- leek pâté in its loaf pan, wrapped in plastic wrap
- chopped vegetables for soup in a self-sealing plastic bag
- salad in a covered bowl
- pears in a rigid container
- vacuum bottle of cold soup
- blue cheese cut in wedges, in a self-sealing plastic bag

BASKET

- vacuum bottle of coffee
- baguette
- dishes and utensils
- tablecloth

TO BUY ON THE WAY

- wine

After you've toured the historical exhibits, tasted the wines, and selected one for the picnic, put the tablecloth on a table and set out the plates and silverware. Serve everyone some cold tomato bouillon with the vegetables sprinkled on top. Open the wine and unmold the pâté. After it's sliced and served and you've dug down through the salad for everyone, cut the baguette and pass that. As you sip whatever wine you've chosen, you can be grateful to Count Haraszthy who brought all those wonderful little vines to America so many years ago.

Spring Lake County Park 28

Six miles east of Santa Rosa on Highway 12. Exit west on Los Alamos Road, turn right on Melita Drive, and follow the sign right at the Y intersection. Tables, barbecues, restrooms, water, Entrance fee $2 on summer weekends.

At Spring Lake Park you can picnic, swim, rent a paddle boat or canoe, or go fishing. If you're visiting the wine country on a hot summer day, the lake is a most welcome sight. Actually two small lakes, one for swimming, one for boating, surrounded with patches of green lawn, make up the park. Willow trees droop into the water, and families of ducks will look enquiringly at your picnic.

If you find Spring Lake Park too crowded, or if you prefer a more primitive setting for your picnic, take the left fork at Melita Drive and follow the signs to adjacent Annadel State Park. Annadel has a few picnic tables near the parking lot, but it is undeveloped. If you like to hike, take the Lake Trail up to Lake Ilsanjo. You're sure to find a pleasant spot to lunch somewhere in the just under five thousand acres of park.

Another very pleasant park in this same area is Sugarloaf Ridge State Park, which has a picnic area near a creek. To find it, take Adobe Canyon Road east from Highway 12 just north of Kenwood.

Whichever spot you choose, the following picnic is easy to carry and serve. You can make it even easier, of course, by stopping in Sonoma to pick up some food. (See Picnic 26.) If you have time to do some advance planning, you'll find this picnic delicious.

Spring Lake Mandarin Menu

PINEAPPLE SPEARS

MANDARIN PORK

SOFT ROLLS

COLESLAW WITH MUSTARDY MAYONNAISE

GRAPES

BEAUJOLAIS OR WHITE ZINFANDEL
(OR A WINE YOU'VE TASTED AND LIKED)

NUT COOKIES

COFFEE

MANDARIN PORK

This recipe serves eight. Extra servings can be frozen and used for hors d'oeuvres.

One 5-pound pork butt, sliced against the grain and cut into pieces
4 tablespoons hoisin sauce
5 tablespoons catsup
1 cup sugar
4 tablespoons soy sauce
2 teaspoons saltpeter (buy at a drug store)
5 tablespoons honey
2 tablespoons toasted sesame seeds

Combine all the ingredients except the honey and sesame seeds. Marinate the pork in the sauce at least 6 hours. Bake it on a rack in the oven at 400°F. for 30 to 40 minutes. Warm the honey and pour it over the finished pork.

Bring the sesame seeds to the picnic in a separate container, and sprinkle over the meat just before serving. To eat, break open a soft roll and put the pork inside. Serves 8.

COLESLAW WITH MUSTARDY MAYONNAISE

Cut Chinese cabbage into thin crosswise slices. To ½ cup mayonnaise (homemade is best) add 2 tablespoons Dijon-style mustard, a dash of pepper, and 1 tablespoon lemon juice. Mix with the cabbage and pack in a lidded container. Serves 4.

Packing Up

CHECK LIST B

COOLER

- ✓ pork in a covered container
- ✓ coleslaw in a covered container
- ✓ grapes in a rigid container
- ✓ pineapple in a covered container

BASKET

- ✓ cookies in a tin or other rigid container
- ✓ vacuum bottle of coffee
- ✓ rolls in a sack
- ✓ plates and utensils

TO BUY ON THE WAY

- ✓ wine

If you've elected to hike a bit to a picnic site, bring along day packs and transfer the food at the parking lot. When you've settled on a spot, serve everyone some pork and some cole-slaw. Pass the soft rolls for tucking the pork into. Open up the wine you've selected on your tasting expedition and enjoy your Sonoma Valley surroundings.

Cuvaison Winery   29

From Highway 29 north of St. Helena, take Dunaweal Lane east to the Silverado Trail and turn south (right); the winery is on the east side. Tasting room open Wednesday through Sunday. You may picnic or purchase a bottle of wine at the office any day of the week. Tables, water, restrooms.

Cuvaison is a relatively new winery housed in a hand-some Spanish colonial–style building. The Silverado side of the Napa Valley is much more sparsely settled than the Highway 29 route, though traffic can be pretty dense on busy weekend, as many people know of this alternate way through the valley. Any number of roads, from the Oakville Cross in the south to Tubbs Lane north of Calistoga, will take you across to this parallel route.

At Cuvaison, you can picnic at tables under um-brellas on the attractive patio of the tasting room, or on other tables located on a grassy expanse in front of the winery or under an oak tree up the hill from the parking lot. Though the picnic areas are smaller than those at either Hacienda or Buena Vista, they are also less frequented, so your chances for a peaceful picnic are good.

The manager of the winery explained to me that they have a picnic area because they know people appreciate it, and that because the winery is small and somewhat out of the way, they have not found it too much trouble to maintain.

The best of the Cuvaison wines, in my opinion, are the Chardonnays and the Zinfandels, especially the '74s or '75s, which would go well with our picnic. If the tasting room is closed, make your way up the hill to the office where you can buy a bottle of your choice.

Cuvaison Winery Cold Beef Collation

FETA CHEESE ROLLED IN CHIVES

THIN SLICES OF COLD ROAST BEEF

FRESH RYE BREAD & SWEET BUTTER

ASSORTMENT OF MUSTARDS

CAPONATA

GINGERBREAD

ZINFANDEL

COFFEE

FETA CHEESE ROLLED IN CHIVES

Cut about ¼ pound of feta cheese into cubes. Roll in finely chopped fresh chives or green onion tops. Serves 4.

ASSORTMENT OF MUSTARDS

Start with a good, basic French mustard. Put about ¼ cup in each of three small containers with lids. To one, add 1 teaspoon capers, slightly crushed with a little of their juice. To the second, add 1 tablespoon red wine, and squeeze a clove of garlic through a garlic press over the top. To the third, add 2 tablespoons of prepared horseradish.

CAPONATA

1 medium eggplant, peeled and cut in cubes
⅓ cup oil
1 medium onion, chopped
1 clove garlic, crushed
½ cup chopped celery
One 1-pound can tomatoes, cut up
¼ cup sliced pitted black olives
2 tablespoons red wine vinegar
1½ teaspoons salt
1½ teaspoons sugar

Sauté the eggplant in the hot oil in a large skillet until softened and browned, about 10 minutes. Remove with a slotted spoon; set aside. Sauté the onion and garlic until tender. Add the remaining ingredients and the eggplant and simmer, uncovered, 20 minutes. Chill several hours or overnight. Pack in a jar with a lid. Serves 4.

Packing Up

CHECK LIST B

COOLER

- ✓ cheese rolled in chives, in a container with a lid
- ✓ sliced beef on a rimmed dish covered with plastic wrap
- ✓ sweet butter on a covered serving dish
- ✓ caponata in a covered container
- ✓ mustards

BASKET

- ✓ fresh rye bread, sliced and wrapped
- ✓ gingerbread, cut in servings and wrapped
- ✓ vacuum bottle of coffee
- ✓ plates and utensils
- ✓ tablecloth

TO BUY ON THE WAY

- ✓ wine

When you've chosen the very best table under the very best oak tree, spread out the tablecloth and set the places. Everything can be arranged in the center of the table for people to help themselves while you uncork the wine and serve it. If you've been wine tasting, you'll notice how much better the wine tastes as an accompaniment to food! When food and wine are combined with this pleasant place and good company, Omar the Tentmaker is proved right once again: paradise enow!

Yountville City Park and Napa Valley

30

Take the Yountville exit from Highway 29 north of Napa. Go east to Washington, then north two blocks to the park. Tables, barbecues, water.

Yountville is at the southern edge of the Napa Valley wine country. Over on the Silverado Trail you'll find Stag's Leap and Clos de Val a little farther south, but

Domaine Chandon in Yountville is the first winery you come to on Highway 29 north of Napa. I like to begin a winery tour here sipping sparkling wine on the terrace of this very European winery. Unlike most tasting rooms, Domaine Chandon exacts a modest fee for your sample, but it includes a generous glass of what would be called champagne if you were in France, some French bread, and some cheese. Besides, you can enjoy lovely ambience, looking out over the green or golden hills dotted with oak trees. The restaurant here is famous, but please remember that we're going on a picnic!

After getting off to a good start at Domaine Chandon, go east under the freeway to the Yountville specialty-shop complex to pick up the picnic supplies. At the Kitchen Store Delicatessen you can buy cheese, meats, fruit drinks or wine, bread, and napkins. The Vintage Sweet Shop sells candies and ice cream, but it also has sandwiches to go. By all means, make your way across the patio to the Court of the Two Sisters for your choice of expensive-but-worth-it desserts: All of the specialty shops carry wine. Then take your collection of goodies on to the Yountville Park.

If you've arrived in Yountville too early for lunch, you can continue on up to Saint Helena, which has a small but charming city park at the north end of town. There is even a bandstand, which is perfect for picnicking on rainy days. Stop at the Oakville Grocery in Oakville (east side of the highway) for a slice of chicken or rabbit pâté, some Black Forest ham, cornichons, pickled herring, or a dessert such as walnut torte or baklava. This is the parent store of the Oakville Grocery on Pacific Avenue in San Francisco, and it has wonderful delicacies including special mustards, herbs such as "Dalamatian Sage," and chestnut flour and Chinese pine nuts.

Still farther north on Highway 29 (four miles from Saint Helena) is Bothe Napa Valley State Park, where you can swim on summer weekends. The picnic area for day use is unpleasantly close to the road, however, and can be rather noisy, even though you are shaded by wonderful old redwood trees. If the park is not crowded, take the road up to the campground area where you'll find quieter spots complete with rest-rooms, water, and barbecues. As you climb the hill, the vegetation changes quickly to madrone forest, equally beautiful but very different from the redwoods below. (The Bale Grist Mill Historical Monument, which was a popular place for years, has been closed for some time.)

North of Calistoga on Tubbs Lane between Highway 29 and Highway 128 are two interesting spots. Château Montelena Winery has a lovely picnic area with two miniature lakes, but so popular is this place that it is almost always spoken for. You must call well in advance if you wish to use it.

If you've not seen the geyser just east of Calistoga, picnic tables are provided at the site of this natural wonder so you can entertain yourself while you wait for it to spout. The surroundings are not particularly lovely, but the geyser itself is fun to see and it erupts quite faithfully every forty minutes or so. The geyser site is open from 9 to 5 and costs two dollars each for adults.

Yountville Wine-Tasters' Choice

THIS MENU IS UP TO YOU:
WHATEVER CATCHES YOUR FANCY

Packing Up

CHECK LIST A

If you also bring some glasses for wine, a jug of water, a vacuum bottle of coffee with cups, and some napkins, you'll be all set for elegant eating in the surroundings of your choice.

Pacing is everything on a wine tour, so don't try to visit all the wineries on one day, and take time to enjoy a leisurely outdoor meal.

Picnics
for
Pickers

Contra Loma Regional Park

31

From Highway 4 one mile south of Antioch, turn south on Lone Tree Way to Fredrickson Lane. Tables, barbecues, restrooms, water, swimming beach. Parking fee $2.

At almost any time of the year, something is ripe and ready to be picked in California. A picnic is a great way to finish up a fruit-picking (or oyster-buying or pumpkin- or Christmas-tree–selecting) trip. Five areas around the Bay make good food-gathering expeditions: the San Mateo coast, where you'll find pumpkins in the fall, fruits and vegetables during the summer, and Christmas trees in the winter; Sonoma County with its blueberries and Gravenstein apples; and Brentwood in Contra Costa County, Santa Clara County, and Yolo/Solano counties with their cherries, apricots, peaches, and other tree fruits and vegetables.

You can get information about these areas from several sources. My earlier book, *Picked This Morning*, will tell you about growers throughout the state, help you plan a trip, advise you about what to do with the food when you get it home, and, of course, tell you where to picnic.

The state Department of Food and Agriculture has a Direct Marketing Program with a toll-free number, (800) 952-5272, which you can call to request their Farmer-to-Consumer Directory listing farmers throughout the state. Growers in some areas have grouped together to print maps showing the locations of their farms, and will send one for a self-addressed stamped envelope. Five of these farm trails organizations and their addresses are:

Harvest Time in
  Brentwood
P.O. Box O
Brentwood, CA 94513

County Crossroads
1369 North Fourth Street
San Jose, CA 95112

Sonoma County Farm
   Trails
P.O. Box 6043
Santa Rosa, CA 95046

Napa County Farming
   Trails
4075 Solano Avenue
Napa, CA 94558

Yolano Farm Trails
P.O. Box 484
Winters, CA 95694

Brentwood is a splendid place to find tree fruits, as well as berries, nuts, and fresh vegetables including sticky-fresh sweet corn. A morning spent picking your favorite fruit, followed by a stop at a stand for whatever other fruits and vegetables you want, will leave you ready for a picnic site where you can plunge into a refreshingly cool lake for a restorative swim. Contra Loma Park is a relatively new area that has already undergone some expansion. It even uses solar heating for its hot water.

   After you've found a table and had a cooling swim, you can eat some of the produce you gathered while it's still at its freshest and best.

Brentwood Fresh-Food Bonanza

SLICED TOMATOES SPRINKLED WITH OIL AND BASIL

CHEESE AND SAUSAGE BOARD

RYE BREAD, BAGUETTE

FRESHLY PICKED FRUIT WITH PORT

NUTS

BEAUJOLAIS OR BEER

COFFEE

CHEESE AND SAUSAGE BOARD

Bring an assortment of cheeses such as Brie or Camembert, Gouda or Danish Havarti, some type of Cheddar. For sausage, try Italian salami, German summer sausage, and liverwurst. For best quality, bring cheeses and meats in the cooler and slice them at the picnic.

FRESHLY PICKED FRUIT WITH PORT

Bring along about ½ cup of port wine in a large container with a lid. When you arrive at the picnic site, wash some of the ripest fruit you picked and slice it into the port to marinate while you eat the rest of the picnic.

Packing Up

TO CHECK LIST B, ADD:

- a nutcracker
- an extra cutting board or wooden tray on which to arrange the cheese and sausage

COOLER

- cheeses wrapped in plastic wrap
- sausage wrapped in plastic wrap
- port in a large container with a lid
- container of salad or olive oil
- basil, fresh or dried, in a plastic bag
- beer

BASKET

- bread
- salt and pepper
- coffee in a vacuum bottle
- wine
- plates and utensils

TO BUY ON THE WAY

- tomatoes
- selection of fruit
- almonds or walnuts
- vegetables

After you have set the picnic table, wash the fruit and cut it into the port. Slice the tomatoes, purchased at a farm or stand, and sprinkle them with the olive oil, basil, and some salt and pepper. Cut the bread and slice the sausage. Let people cut their own pieces of cheese. If you've bought other fresh vegetables, have a few of those while they're still crisp and tender. You can buy both almonds and walnuts in Brentwood to have with fruit for dessert. You'll find that fruits and vegetables eaten so soon after picking have a special taste that will make this simple meal a memorable one.

Tomales Bay State Park

32

From Highway 1, two miles north of Olema, take Sir Francis Drake Boulevard to the left. In approximately eight miles, look for the sign to Johnson's Oyster Farm to the left. To reach Tomales Bay State Park, retrace your route along Sir Francis Drake Boulevard to Pierce Point Road, the first turn to your left. Tables, barbecues, restrooms, water. Day use fee $2.

Mounds of oyster shells higher than your head will herald your approach to Johnson's Oyster Farm off Sir Francis Drake Boulevard near the park. Here you can pick up fresh oysters for your beach barbecue. The cool temperatures of Drakes Bay make oysters safe to eat all year long, so you can buy them during any month. To order your oysters in advance, you can telephone (415) 669-1149. In the Petaluma area you can also buy oysters at the Buchan Oyster Company, 1105 Bodega Avenue, telephone (707) 763-4161; open daily from 9 to 5.

Oysters are farmed by using strings of old oyster shells to which the young are attached. These strings are then tied to the cross pieces of the picket-fencelike structures that you see sticking up from the shallow water. After the "spat" have matured into young oysters, the shells are unstrung and thrown onto the muddy sand. A year later, the old shells are shattered, freeing each cluster of young oysters to grow.

After you've picked up your oysters (how many will depend on the appetite of your group) you must decide whether to go back to Tomales Bay State Park and one of the beaches there, or to continue on Sir Francis Drake Boulevard through Point Reyes National Seashore. Your choice may well depend on the weather. If it's too foggy or chilly to enjoy the ocean side, opt for the more sheltered spots at Tomales Bay. I like Heart's Desire Beach. (Maybe it's just the name!) If you have children along, the water here is calm and shallow—safe for paddling while you prepare the feast.

Tomales Bay Oyster Barbecue

CLEAR MUSHROOM SOUP

BARBECUED OYSTERS

CORN ON THE COB OR SKEWERED VEGETABLES

SLICED TOMATOES

CHAMPAGNE OR CHENIN BLANC

FRENCH APPLE AND PEAR CAKE

COFFEE

CLEAR MUSHROOM SOUP

¾ pound mushrooms,
    rinsed
3 green onions with tops
4 cups chicken broth
1 piece fresh ginger, about
    1 inch in diameter and 1
    inch long, thinly sliced

Soy sauce to taste
Salt to taste
Thin lime slices
Sprigs of coriander
    (optional)

Reserve about one third of the smaller mushrooms. Mince
the remainder with the onions and the ginger, either by hand
or in a food processor, with 1½ cups of the broth. Transfer to a
pot, and add the remaining broth. Simmer, partly covered, for
20 minutes. Strain through a sieve. Slice the reserved mushrooms very thin and add to the soup. Bring to a simmer and
add the soy sauce and salt.

Pour into a large vacuum bottle to transport to the picnic.
Serve in mugs, garnished with the lime slices and coriander if
you like it. Serves 4.

CORN ON THE COB OR SKEWERED VEGETABLES

If it's fresh corn season, bring 1 or 2 ears per person. Carefully
pull back the husks and gently remove the silk (and any
insect life). Pull the husks back up. At the picnic, roast the
ears on the barbecue in the husks. After about 10 minutes on
the barbecue, turn it and cook another 10 minutes. Some
heavy gloves will help you to husk it while it's hot. Test for
doneness by pricking with a fork.

If corn is not in season, bring some small skewers of fresh
vegetables such as Brussels sprouts, squash, onions, and
cherry tomatoes. These will cook in about 10 minutes.

FRENCH APPLE AND PEAR CAKE

This is a firm cake that requires no frosting and travels well.

2 large eggs
¾ cup sugar
¾ cup all-purpose sifted flour
½ cup plus 1 tablespoon unsalted butter, softened
⅛ teaspoon salt

2 apples, peeled, cored and sliced thin
2 pears, peeled, cored, and sliced thin
1 tablespoon baking powder
1½ teaspoons light rum

Beat the eggs with the sugar until the mixture is light and lemon colored. Add the flour, softened butter, and salt and beat well. Stir in the apples and pears, then baking powder and rum.

Spoon the batter into a well-buttered and -sugared 9-inch round cake pan. Bake at 325°F. for 35 minutes or until a tester inserted in the center comes out clean. Cool in the pan on a rack for 30 minutes before removing the cake from the pan. Serves 6 to 8.

Packing Up

TO CHECK LIST C, ADD:

- ✓ mugs for the soup
- ✓ heavy gloves for handling the corn and oysters
- ✓ a dish for melting butter

- ✓ bucket for water in which to scrub the oysters
- ✓ a sharp knife for each person

COOLER

- ✓ corn or vegetable skewers wrapped in plastic wrap
- ✓ tomatoes, sliced and put in a rimmed dish with a lid

- ✓ wine
- ✓ butter for the corn and oysters in an ovenproof dish

BASKET

- ✓ vacuum bottle of soup
- ✓ vacuum bottle of coffee
- ✓ cake well wrapped in plastic wrap

- ✓ Worcestershire sauce
- ✓ Tabasco sauce
- ✓ plates and utensils
- ✓ salt and pepper

EXTRA SACK

- ✓ charcoal, starter, and matches
- ✓ any other equipment that hasn't fit in elsewhere

(this sack may fit in the bucket if you're bringing a large one)

TO BUY ON THE WAY

✓ oysters in the shell (at
   least 6 per person)

After you've picked up the oysters and found a good spot for
the barbecue, get a good hot charcoal fire going and let it burn
down until the coals are covered with a thin coating of ash.
Meanwhile, serve the clear mushroom soup. In the bucket,
scrub the oysters and make sure they are all closed. (Discard
any that are open.) Put the oysters on the grill very close to
the coals and leave them for about 10 minutes, or until the
shells start to open. You'll have to pry them open the rest of
the way, but it's not very hard. When they're done (you may
want to do them in several batches) serve them on plates.
Pass a sauce made by heating some butter in a Pyrex dish over
the coals and adding Worcestershire and Tabasco sauce. If you
have room on the fire, cook the corn or vegetables at the same
time; otherwise cook oysters, then corn or vegetables in
batches. The empty shells can go in the bucket. If you prefer a
barbecue sauce, bring that instead of the butter. Have lots of
napkins! Everyone can wash off in the bay when the feast is
over.

San Gregorio Beach State Park 33

*Ten and a half miles south of Half Moon Bay on Highway 1,
at the junction with Highway 84. Tables, barbecues, restrooms. No water.*

Just before Halloween, Half Moon Bay is often over-
run with people who have come to buy pumpkins
from the many farms that spread over the shallow
coastal plain. If you don't mind crowds, or you can
come during the week, pumpkin buying is fun to do.
At other times of the year you can find fresh fruits and
vegetables at stands, and at Christmas time, you can
choose and cut a tree from one of several Christmas
tree farms. See Picnic 31 for details on how to find
farms and stands.

A series of creeks empties into the ocean along the San Mateo coast. Many of the beaches created by the creeks are part of the state park system and are good places to picnic after collecting some straight-from-the-farm produce. From Pacifica south, Gray Whale Cove Beach is the first one you reach, followed by Montara. The parking here is quite limited. James V. Fitzgerald Marine Reserve in Moss Beach is not a state beach, but it's a very good picnic place, described in Picnic 13. The beach at Half Moon Bay is very extensive and quite open. On the level areas around Dunes Beach you'll find a good display of California poppies in the spring.

Below Half Moon Bay are San Gregorio, Pompano, and Pescadero state beaches. At Pescadero you'll find a long sweep of beach for running or beachcombing, and a landside trail around an inlet that is good for birding. My favorite among these beaches, however, is San Gregorio. Cliffs at either end and a dramatic lone cypress tree at the top of one cliff give it a special scenic quality. It's also of historic interest, as Portola and his men camped here in October 1769 during the journey that culminated in the discovery of San Francisco Bay. They had missed Monterey Bay, and they stayed at San Gregorio several days to rest and care for their sick. A monument near the entrance to the beach commemorates this visit.

Weather here is often cold and/or foggy, so this picnic will help keep you warm as you explore the beach. This picnic serves six people.

San Gregorio Black Bean Soup Repast

CARIBBEAN BLACK BEAN SOUP

COOKED MEAT AND CORN SALAD

HARD ROLLS & BUTTER

HOT CHOCOLATE

COFFEE & WATER

PICNIC PUMPKIN FLAN

CARIBBEAN BLACK BEAN SOUP

2 cups dried black beans	¼ teaspoon dried thyme
2 quarts cold water	⅛ teaspoon dried
1 onion, chopped	marjoram
1 clove garlic	1 bay leaf
1 ham bone, or 2 ham hocks	Pinch ground coriander
1 teaspoon dried oregano	Salt to taste
½ teaspoon ground cumin	Chopped onion

Soak the beans in water to cover overnight or follow package directions. Drain the beans and add cold water. Add the remaining ingredients except the onion garnish and simmer, partially covered, for 3–4 hours, or until the beans are soft, adding more water if necessary. Remove the ham bone and purée the beans in a blender or processor or beat by hand.

Get the soup very hot and put it in a wide-mouthed vacuum bottle to carry it to the picnic. To serve, pass a small bowl of the chopped onion to sprinkle on top of the soup. Serves 6.

COOKED MEAT AND CORN SALAD

2 cups cold cooked meat, cut in strips	1 small red onion, sliced in rings
Dressing, following	One 17-ounce can whole-kernel corn, drained
3 cups shredded cabbage	
1 green pepper, seeded and cut into short slivers	¼ cup chopped fresh cilantro
2 tomatoes, diced	2 hard-cooked eggs

Marinate the meat in the dressing, following, for about an hour. Add all the remaining ingredients except the eggs. Bring the eggs to the picnic whole and slice them for garnish just before serving. Serves 6.

Dressing

Stir together ½ cup oil, ⅓ cup red wine vinegar, 1 teaspoon chili powder, 1½ teaspoons garlic salt, and ¼ teaspoon crushed dried red pepper.

PICNIC PUMPKIN FLAN

A real flan would be coated with carmelized sugar and unmolded, but this is eaten right out of the cup.

Grated zest of 1 lemon	2 tablespoons sugar
1½ cups milk	¼ cup dark rum
½ cup heavy cream	¼ teaspoon salt
¾ cup canned or fresh pumpkin purée	3 eggs
	2 egg yolks
⅓ cup honey	

In a heavy saucepan, combine the lemon zest, milk, and cream. Bring to just under a simmer, stirring often. Remove from heat and cover. To the pumpkin purée, add the honey, sugar, rum, and salt and beat. Blend the eggs and yolks in a separate bowl, then strain into the purée and mix. Strain in the milk, stirring constantly.

Pour the custard into 6 lightly buttered individual oven-proof cups. Set them in a pan of water to come halfway up the sides and cover with aluminum foil. Bake 20 minutes at 325°F. Remove the foil. Continue baking until the custard is set and a knife inserted in the center comes out clean. Cover with plastic wrap and chill. Makes 6 servings.

Packing Up

TO CHECK LIST B, ADD:

- ✔ bowls or mugs for soup
- ✔ soup spoons

COOLER

- ✔ salad in a covered container
- ✔ hard-cooked eggs in a rigid container
- ✔ butter for the rolls in a self-sealing plastic bag
- ✔ small container of chopped onion for soup garnish

BASKET

- ✔ vacuum bottle of soup (or wrap heavy pot with towels, newspaper)
- ✔ vacuum bottles of coffee and chocolate
- ✔ rolls in a sack
- ✔ pumpkin flan in individual molds
- ✔ plates, bowls, and utensils

When you've explored the historic monument and had a jog on the beach, find a table and serve everyone some soup and salad. Pass the rolls and butter and the soup garnish. The warm, spicy food should take away any chill from the ocean fog or breezes.

Solano Creek County Park   **34**

From Highway 128 three miles west of Winters, take Pleasants Valley Road south (toward Vacaville). The park extends across the road on both sides. Swimming access on east side. Tables, barbecues, restrooms, water, playground.

Yolo and Solano counties are most often thought of as summer fruit- and nut-growing territory, and so they are. Wonderful cherries, apricots, and peaches grow here, along with almonds, walnuts, and other fruits and vegetables. But surprisingly enough, another crop that you can get directly from the growers in this area is oranges. Commercial groves were once thick around Sacramento, and most farmhouses hereabouts still have a few orange trees on the grounds. Oranges are grown commercially even farther north around Oroville, and the so-called Mother Orange Tree grew there from 1856 to 1960, when it was moved to make way for the Oroville Dam.

Oranges ripen toward the end of February and into March, so an early spring excursion to this northern Suisun Bay region can make a wonderful day, especially if you choose one with bright blue, beautiful skies. See Picnic 31 for details on how to find the farms.

You'll probably want to come in the summer, too, and Solano Creek Park with its swimming and boating facilities makes an appealing place for a picnic, whether you just want to have lunch or can use a cooling swim. A large, shady park extends along the creek, and you can use one of the park's tables or spread your picnic out under one of the trees. You can buy snacks or cold drinks here if you like.

Because these fruit-picking trips are fun for a family or a group of friends, here's a picnic to appeal to children as well as adults. This picnic is designed to serve eight.

Solano Fried Chicken Family Feast

OVEN-FRIED CHICKEN

PARTY MACARONI

ROLLS

CELERY STUFFED WITH PEANUT BUTTER AND
CREAM CHEESE

FRESH FRUIT

GREEN HUNGARIAN OR DRY SEMILLON

LEMONADE

CHOCOLATE CUPCAKES

COFFEE

OVEN-FRIED CHICKEN

2 frying chickens, cut
  up (best pieces)
1 cup flour
1 teaspoon salt
1 teaspoon seasoned salt
½ teaspoon dried tarragon
¼ teaspoon ground nutmeg
½ teaspoon pepper
½ cup milk

Wash and dry the chicken. Put all the remaining ingredients
except the milk in a paper sack and gently shake to mix. Dip
the chicken in the milk, then shake a few pieces at a time in
the seasoned flour to coat.

    Place on a cookie sheet in a single layer. Bake at 400°F. for
45 minutes to an hour. (If you line the pans with aluminum
foil, oil it lightly to prevent sticking.) Serves 8.

PARTY MACARONI

One 8-ounce package elbow
  macaroni
One 10-ounce package
  frozen peas
½ cup chopped celery
¼ cup grated onion
2 pimientos, chopped
2 teaspoons chopped fresh
  or dried dill
1 cup White Sauce,
  following
1½ cups buttered coarse
  bread crumbs

Cook the macaroni in a large kettle of boiling water until it is
tender. Add the frozen peas during the last 3 minutes. Drain.
Combine with all the remaining ingredients except the

crumbs and place in a 3-quart shallow baking dish. Top with the buttered crumbs. Bake at 350°F. for 30 minutes. Serve hot or cold. Serves 8.

White Sauce

In a saucepan, melt 2 tablespoons butter. Stir in 1½ table-spoons flour, 1 teaspoon salt, and ⅛ teaspoon pepper. Gradually stir in 1 cup of milk and bring to the boil. Boil 1 minute, stirring constantly.

Packing Up

CHECK LIST B

COOLER

- ✓ chicken in a covered container
- ✓ macaroni in a covered bowl
- ✓ stuffed celery in a self-sealing plastic bag
- ✓ fruit in a rigid container
- ✓ butter for rolls
- ✓ wine

If you want to take the macaroni hot, wrap it in a towel or several layers of newspaper. The chicken will also stay hot this way, and it will present no danger if it is thoroughly cooked.

BASKET

- ✓ rolls in a sack
- ✓ cupcakes in a box, wrapped with plastic
- ✓ vacuum bottle of lemonade
- ✓ vacuum bottle of coffee
- ✓ plates and utensils

TO BUY ON THE WAY

- ✓ fruits, nuts and/or vegetables

Depending on the time of year you choose, you may go for a swim or have a brisk trot around the park, to either cool off or warm up before you eat. When you've achieved about the right temperature, spread out the food, and let everyone help himself. Be sure to add some of whatever bounty you've been picking.

Ed R. Levin County Park

35

At the junction of Highway 680 and 237 just north of Milpitas, take Calaveras Road east and follow the signs to the park. Tables, barbecues, restrooms, water.

Santa Clara County had the first commercial agricul-tural area in California, planted in the 1850s to help feed the rush of population that came with the discovery of gold. Not all of the riches that came out of the ground were metal. In spite of the growing overlay of housing developments, you can still find little farms where you can buy fruit, eggs, and fresh vegetables directly from the farmer. See Picnic 31 for information on finding the growers' locations.

Historically, the most important crop in this valley has been the prune. All prunes are plums, but not all plums are prunes: the difference is that a prune can be dried with the seed still inside without fermenting. If you've never tried drying fruit, you might want to buy some fresh prunes and see for yourself how it works.

From the northeast peach and pear growing area of San Jose, a good picnic destination is Ed R. Levin County Park.

As you approach the park, take the left turn to Sandy Wool Lake and follow the road around the shore to the parking area at the far end. Here you'll find shaded tables along the water's edge. Unfortunately, no swimming or wading is allowed, but you can enjoy the cool breezes across the water. If the fruit picking hasn't tired you out too much, you can walk around the lake or take one of the trails over the hills to help you work up an appetite for a cool, refreshing fruit salad lunch.

Santa Clara Fruit Salad Refreshment

FOUR-FRUIT SALAD WITH CHOICE OF DRESSINGS

SHOESTRING POTATOES

HAM SLICES

ROLLS

FRENCH MUSTARD

SEMILLON OR SYLVANER

COFFEE

FOUR-FRUIT SALAD

If you are planning to pick fruit, you can use some of it for this salad. Plan to buy other fruits at a stand along the way to combine with a choice of dressings, or bring fruit from home. Choose at least 4 kinds, keeping the colors in mind for a pretty effect. Bring a little parsley to decorate each plate. You'll need 2 pieces of large fruits such as pears or peaches combined with 1 cup of small fruits to serve 4. At the picnic site, wash the fruit and cut it into large chunks, arranging it on the plate as you go so everyone gets an equal selection. You can bring lettuce leaves to put under it if you like. Let people help themselves to one of the following dressings.

Lime Dressing

¼ cup oil
2 tablespoons lime juice
¼ teaspoon Tabasco sauce

2 teaspoons sugar
¼ teaspoon pepper
Salt to taste

Combine all the ingredients in a jar with a tight-fitting lid. Shake until blended. Carry to the picnic in the jar.

Nut Dressing

20 whole blanched almonds
¼ teaspoon dry mustard
¼ teaspoon paprika
½ teaspoon catsup

¼ teaspoon sugar
1 tablespoon vinegar
Salt to taste
5 tablespoons oil

Grind the nuts in a blender to pulverize. Add all the remaining ingredients except the oil. Blend. Slowly add the oil, with the blender lid off.

Honey-Yogurt Dressing

½ cup plain yogurt
1 tablespoon white vinegar
1 tablespoon lemon juice

Dash pepper
2 tablespoons honey
Salt to taste

Combine all the ingredients in a bowl and blend until well mixed. Refrigerate.

Packing Up

TO CHECK LIST B, ADD:

🗸 a peeler

COOLER

🗸 lettuce leaves, washed and dried, in a plastic sack
🗸 ham slices in a self-sealing plastic bag

🗸 mustard
🗸 assorted salad dressings in jars with tight lids
🗸 wine

BASKET

🗸 shoestring potatoes
🗸 rolls in a sack

🗸 vacuum bottle of coffee
🗸 plates and utensils

TO BUY ON THE WAY

🗸 fruit

An extremely easy picnic to prepare and serve, this one requires minimum advance preparation, especially if you use a commercial dressing for the salad! When everyone has admired the lake, and perhaps watched a hang-glider being launched nearby, you can wash and prepare the fruit. Set out the rest of the food and relax in this pleasant lakeside setting.

Picnics amid the Flowers

Morgan Territory Regional Preserve 36

Off Morgan Territory Road between Livermore and Clayton. From Livermore, take North Livermore Avenue to Manning Road, turn west, then turn north on Morgan Territory Road and drive 9.4 miles to the park. From Clayton, take Marsh Creek Road to Morgan Territory Road, 13.6 miles to the park. No tables, no barbecues (fires strictly prohibited), no restrooms, no water. Undeveloped.

Wild flowers flourish in all the parks in the Bay Area in the spring, but at Morgan Territory the abundance and variety are astounding. A list compiled in April of 1978 has over seventy kinds of flowers, including yarrow, woodland star, red maids, sticky monkey flower, shooting star, blue gilia, baby blue eyes, and rusty popcorn flower.

Bring your binoculars, too, as the bird life is equally interesting.

Morgan Territory is named for the pioneer family that first settled this beautiful canyon, and there are still some Morgans living here. The park, a relatively recent acquisition of the park district, is used principally by groups of hikers who come to enjoy wilderness close to home.

As you approach the park, watch carefully for the entrance to the east. The parking area is just up the rise near the old farmhouse that serves as a caretaker's home. Because it is a wilderness park, the trails are minimally marked, and you are pretty much on your own to find your way around. With 1,500 acres to wander in, it helps to remember that the ridgeline runs north and south along the canyon. The flowers will be at their best in April, and you'll find ponds and streams to picnic by.

Bring along some trail mix and some jerky to nibble as you look for flowers. When you're ready for lunch, here is a hikers' special to put in your day pack.

Morgan Territory Pocket Bread Picnic

POCKET BREAD

HOMMOS (CHICK-PEA SAUCE)

CUBED MEATS, TOMATOES, LETTUCE, CILANTRO

ASSORTED FRESH VEGETABLES

HARD-COOKED EGGS

FRESH FRUIT

TOASTED ALMOND CAKE

LEMONADE

HOMMOS (CHICK-PEA SAUCE)

One 16-ounce can chick-peas (garbanzos)
2 tablespoons chopped parsley
3 tablespoons sesame oil
¼ cup lemon juice
2 teaspoons salt
2 cloves garlic, crushed

Heat the chick-peas with half the juice from the can. Whirl the chick-peas in a blender until smooth. Add the remaining ingredients and whirl until well blended.

Carry this sauce to the picnic in a container with a good lid. It can be used to line the pocket bread, and also as a dip for the vegetables. Serves 4.

CUBED MEATS, TOMATOES, LETTUCE, CILANTRO

Cut any leftover cooked meat into small cubes. You'll need about 2 cups. Add 2 tomatoes, seeded and chopped, and 1 tablespoon of chopped fresh cilantro, if you like the taste. In a separate plastic bag, bring about 1 cup of chopped lettuce. Picnickers can fill pocket bread first with hommos and then with the meat mixture and lettuce.

TOASTED ALMOND CAKE

1½ cups blanched almonds
1 cup butter or margarine, softened
2 cups sugar
1 teaspoon vanilla
2 eggs
4 cups unsifted all-purpose flour
½ teaspoon each baking powder, soda, and salt
¼ teaspoon ground nutmeg
1 cup milk

Spread the almonds in a single layer on a pan and bake at 350°F. for 10 minutes, shaking pan occasionally. Whirl the almonds in a blender until powdery. With a mixer, cream the butter and sugar until fluffy, then add the vanilla and beat in the eggs, one at a time. Stir the flour with the nuts, baking powder, soda, salt, and nutmeg; then add to the creamed mixture alternately with the milk, beating until smooth.

Heavily butter and flour a 10-inch tube pan. Pour in the cake batter and spread evenly. Bake at 325°F. for 1 hour and 20 minutes, or until a wooden skewer inserted in the center comes out clean. Let cool 10 minutes, then invert on a rack. For the picnic, wrap individual portions tightly in plastic wrap. Be generous—this is very good! Makes 10 to 12 servings.

Packing Up

CHECK LIST B

Subtract the corkscrew, silverware, and wineglasses. Add daypacks.

COOLER

- hommos in a container with a lid
- cubed meats, tomatoes, in a self-sealing plastic bag
- lettuce in a self-sealing plastic bag
- fresh vegetables in a self-sealing plastic bag
- hard-cooked eggs in a rigid container
- fresh fruit in a rigid container
- salt

BASKET

- pocket bread in a sack
- cake wrapped in plastic wrap
- plates and utensils
- vacuum bottle or canteen of lemonade

Bring along a wild flower indentification book and a small magnifying glass for those tricky ones. Please don't pick any, even though they are so plentiful.

When you've parked the car, divide the food among the day packs, keeping the trail mix and jerky on top for easy access. Do bring the ground cloth—it can be very damp here in spring—and spread it out on the flower-surrounded spot of your choice. Set out the food, and let each person fill his own pocket bread and peel his own egg (carefully, of course, so the

shells go back out with you). Complete solitude is more read-
ily available in this wilderness preserve than in most East Bay
parks, so let the peace sink in with the sunshine of a lovely
spring day.

U.C. Botanical Garden   37

*From Piedmont Avenue on the east side of the Berkeley
campus, take either Stadium Rim Way or Canyon Road,
east behind the stadium, into Strawberry Canyon. The gardens are on the right. Open daily from 9 to 5. Tables, water,
restrooms. The visitors' center is open Monday and Friday
from 12 to 3, and Tuesday, Wednesday and Thursday from
12:30 to 3:30; weekends from 10 to 4:30.*

A gracefully laid-out garden where every plant can be
immediately identified by its tidy sign may not appeal
to everyone, but for the botanically minded, or the
person who just enjoys seeing a variety of growing
things, such a place can be a great comfort and an
inspiration. In addition to plants arranged by areas of
the world—China Hill, New World Desert—the U.C.
Botanical Garden has a creek and small pool, a rhododendron dell and an herb garden, and—most important of all—a few picnic tables scattered in choice
locations.

The network of paths can take hours to explore. A
good way to start is with the self-guiding Indian Nature Trail, for which you'll need a booklet from the Visitors' Center. You can learn, for example, that Indians
wove the leaves of cattails together to make floor mats
and roof thatches, that the pollen was mixed with
water into little cakes, and that the absorbent down
was used to line cradles. The new shoots were eaten in
spring, and the root stocks were ground up for use
during cold months. And that's just one of the twenty-
nine plants you'll encounter along this path.

Bird lovers should bring binoculars, as the Visitors'
Center also supplies a list of the seventy-six varieties

that have been identified here. Birds must enjoy an occasional exotic snack, too.

Tables are found at four places in the garden. My favorite spot is one located in the redwoods area near the creek. Slightly elevated above the paths, the site is cool and forestlike. More spacious and more secluded is the group of tables near the Californian Area. As you approach the end of the loop through these plant beds, take the little switchback trail to the right; it goes up above the canyon to an oak-shaded overlook where you'll find three tables and even a drinking fountain.

For a site by the creek, stay on the main path around the pool and, just as you cross the creek, take the small trail up to the left. Here you'll be surrounded by Chinese plants including exotic bamboos and camellias.

One more table is located across from the Herb Garden, and it, too, is pleasantly shaded, but not so private as the others. If all the tables are in use, you can climb up to the meadow in the South American Area, where you'll find benches with views out over the Bay, with the Berkeley fishing pier in the foreground. In spring, the meadow is filled with poppies.

This picnic requires only a stop at a market or deli, and it is easy to carry, leaving you free to roam the paths of the garden until you're ready to eat. (Wine is not included on this picnic as you are technically on the grounds of the university.)

U.C. Botanical Plant Person's Avocado-Tuna Salad

AVOCADO-TUNA SALAD

BREAD

BEL PAESE, PROVOLONE, OR GORGONZOLA CHEESE

FRESH FRUIT

FAVORITE COOKIES

COFFEE OR SODA

AVOCADO-TUNA SALAD

2 avocados
1 lemon
One 6½-ounce can tuna

One 8-ounce carton plain
  yogurt

At the picnic site, cut the avocados in half, twist sharply to open, and take out the seeds; peel. Cut the lemon and sprinkle some juice on each avocado half. Open the tuna, drain it into a plastic sack, serve some into each avocado, and sprinkle with more lemon. Top with the yogurt.

Packing Up

TO CHECK LIST B, ADD:

✓ day packs
✓ can opener

Omit the wineglasses and serving spoon.

TO BUY ON THE WAY

✓ can of tuna
✓ 2 avocados
✓ carton of yogurt
✓ bread

✓ cheese
✓ fruit
✓ cookies
✓ soft drink or juice

Pick up a plastic produce bag and an extra paper sack.

The plastic sack is for the tuna oil and can to make disposal easier. When you buy the yogurt, wrap it in an extra paper bag to keep it cool. Upon arrival, divide the food, utensils, and equipment evenly among the days packs and set out for garden exploration.

At the picnic site, prepare the avocado salads, then cut the bread and cheese and pass that. A garden is a lovely thing, and a lovely place to enjoy a simple meal with friends.

Rhododendron Dell, Golden Gate Park   38

The Rhododendron Dell is in the eastern section of Golden Gate Park, south of Kennedy Drive between Sixth and Eighth avenues. Restrooms are in the Conservatory to the east, or the de Young Museum to the west.

John McLaren, the doughty Scot who brought Golden Gate Park into being, loved rhododendrons, and the twenty-acre Rhododendron Dell across from the Conservatory is a testament to his favorite flower. In March or early April when they put on a show that would do credit to the cover of a seed catalog, it's easy to see why he took such delight in these big, showy blossoms.

You may want to make a visit to the Conservatory first, just to marvel at the exotic plants in this amazing greenhouse that came round the Horn, then make your way over to the Rhododendron Dell for a proper Scottish tea in honor of the park's great gardener. It may well be chilly, but the dell is sheltered, and with a warming cup of tea in hand, you should be fine.

Rhododendron Dell Scottish Tea

SCONES WITH TWO KINDS OF JAM

BRIDE'S SLICES

WATERCRESS AND CUCUMBER SANDWICHES

SHARP–CHEDDAR CHEESE STICKS

CHOCOLATE TORTE

EARL GREY TEA

SCONES
(rhymes with 'gone')

4 cups sifted cake flour	¼ cup (½ stick)
1 teaspoon salt	unsalted butter
1 tablespoon baking	1 cup buttermilk
powder	1 egg

Preheat the oven to 450°F. Into a large bowl, sift together the dry ingredients. Cut the butter in, then work it into the flour mixture with your fingers until it's thoroughly worked in. In a small bowl, beat the buttermilk and egg together. Make a well in the center of the flour mixture and pour in about three fourths of the milk mixture. Blend lightly with a fork. Gradually add as much more liquid as necessary to make a soft, cohesive, but not sticky dough.

Turn the dough out onto a floured surface and knead it lightly, about 5 or 6 times, just until it holds together in a ball. Pull off pieces of dough about the size of a golf ball and flatten them with your knuckles into pieces about ½ inch thick. Prick with a fork and cut into rounds with a biscuit cutter, or cut into quarters.

Bake at 450°F. for 10 to 15 minutes on a lightly greased baking sheet. While scones are still warm, wrap them well and put them in an insulated container to stay warm for the picnic. Bring 2 of your favorite jams. Makes about 20.

BRIDE'S SLICES

To your favorite pie crust recipe, add 1 egg yolk. Chill the dough, then roll it out into a rectangle about 12 by 18 and ¼ inch thick. With 2 large spatulas, carefully lift it onto a rimmed baking sheet and trim it to fit. With a spatula, spread the following topping evenly over the pastry.

Bake at 350°F. for 20 to 25 minutes. Remove from oven and immediately sprinkle the remaining 2 tablespoons of sugar over the top. Cool in the pan on a wire rack for 15 to 20 minutes. Cut into bars about 2 by 4 inches. Let cool completely. Place in a cookie tin to transport. Makes about 24.

Topping

¼ cup butter, softened
6 tablespoons superfine sugar
2 eggs, lightly beaten
½ cup glacé cherries, coarsely chopped
2 cups currants or raisins
½ cup graham cracker crumbs

Cream the butter with 4 tablespoons of the sugar until the mixture is fluffy. Beat the eggs in 1 at a time. Mix the remaining ingredients into the butter mixture until evenly distributed.

CHOCOLATE TORTE

Five 1-ounce squares semi-sweet chocolate
¾ cup sugar
¾ cup butter, softened
5 eggs, separated
¾ cup all-purpose sifted flour

Carefully melt the chocolate. Cream the sugar and butter until fluffy. Beat the egg yolks in 1 at a time until light in color. Add the cooled chocolate. Add the flour gradually. Beat the egg whites until stiff but not dry. Gently fold them into chocolate mixture.

Bake in a 9-inch removable-rim pan at 325°F. for 50 to 60 minutes. When cool, cut in slices and wrap individually to carry to the picnic. Makes 8 servings.

Packing Up

CHECK LIST B

Omit the corkscrew and wineglasses.

BASKET

Everything for this picnic can go in a large basket. If the sandwiches are wrapped and chilled, they'll be fine. Put them in a rigid container so they won't be crushed. The scones can be buttered at home while warm. Bring the jams in small containers with lids.

When you've spread out your waterproof ground cloth, set out the tea things. Everyone can help himself. Pour everyone some hot, aromatic tea. You may want to bring lump sugar so you can enquire, "One lump or two?" Do choose a spot where you can admire McLaren's favorite blossoms while you sip and nibble.

Sam McDonald County Park 39

From Highway 84 south of La Honda, take Pescadero Road south. Tables, barbecues, restrooms, water.

People who have parks named after them are usually prominent citizens, wealthy philanthropists, or famous public figures. But Sam McDonald was the son of slave parents. He started work at Standford University in 1903 as a teamster and stayed for fifty years, eventually becoming superintendent of athletic grounds and buildings. He began buying property around La Honda in 1917 and gradually acquired over four hundred acres. When he died, he left the property to Stanford with the stipulation that it become a park. Eventually, the county bought it, added to it, and named it after him: Sam McDonald County Park.

Within the park are two quite separate environments. The section north of Pescadero Road is principally redwood forest, and on the lower elevations here in the moist ravines are many fern varieties: five finger, sword, lady, gold back, and the polypody and woodwardia strains. You'll also find trillium, redwood violet, red clintonia, and wild strawberry. Redwood sorrel and curious kinds of mushrooms are prevalent in spring.

From the drier, open ridges south of the road you can see out to the Pacific Ocean. In spring you'll find sticky monkey flower, wood rose, sun cup, and the lovely and ubiquitous California poppy. You can wander at will, and picnic in either section of the park. Some tables are located near the entrance. Others are at the Haida Center, 2½ miles to the northwest on the Camp Trail. The Towne Cabin site also has tables and water, and is to the southeast on the Towne Trail. Farther along this same trail is a very picturesque hikers' hut. Really dedicated hikers can go all the way to Pescadero Creek Park to the south.

Because the terrain is rather rugged and there are few amenities, you can usually count on a good bit of solitary strolling along the lovely trails. I like lots of reasons to stop and rest when I'm hiking, so this picnic is meant to be consumed in stages (it serves four people).

Sam McDonald Four-Stop Picnic

FIRST STOP:
ORANGES, STRAWBERRIES

SECOND STOP:
BAGELS, LOX, CREAM CHEESE
VEGETABLE STICKS

THIRD STOP:
THIN SLICED RYE BREAD
MUSTARD
BEEF OR HAM
ZINFANDEL

FOURTH STOP:
WORLD'S BEST COOKIES

COFFEE OR WATER AT EACH STOP

WORLD'S BEST COOKIES

Well, *I* like them! These cookies freeze well, or keep well in a cookie tin.

½ cup butter, softened
1 cup packed brown sugar
1 egg
½ teaspoon vanilla
1 ¾ cups sifted cake flour

¼ teaspoon salt
1 teaspoon baking powder
½ cup ground blanched
  almonds

Cream together the butter and sugar until fluffy. Add the egg and the vanilla. Stir the flour, salt, and baking powder together with the almonds. Add gradually to the batter. Chill for at least 2 hours.

Roll out thin on a floured surface and cut into shapes with cookie cutters or a knife. Bake at 350°F. for 8 to 10 minutes. Makes about 40.

Packing Up

TO CHECK LIST B, ADD:

✔ day packs

COOLER

✔ fruit in a rigid container
✔ mustard
✔ all the following in self-sealing plastic bags: lox, ¼ pound; cream cheese, 1 small package; vegetable sticks; sliced meat, ½ pound

BASKET

✔ vacuum bottle of coffee
✔ water container
✔ bread wrapped in plastic wrap
✔ 8 bagels in a self-sealing plastic bag
✔ wine
✔ cookies in a rigid container
✔ plates and utensils

When you've parked the car, divide up the food and equipment among the day packs as fairly as possible. Whichever direction you choose to go, you'll find beautiful places to stop and enjoy the various courses of this hikers' picnic.

Morcom Amphitheatre of Roses

40

From Highway 580 in Oakland, take the Grand Avenue exit east. Go 4 blocks to Jean Street and turn left to the garden entrance. To enter from above, take Oakland Avenue east to Olive Avenue and turn south. Park on Olive Street. Open daily. Restrooms, water. No tables, no barbecues.

I like to approach the Oakland Rose Garden from above, on the Oakland Avenue side, and walk down through the shady redwood grove to the brilliant carpet of roses below. Paths are laid out so that you can't see all of the garden at once, but wandering will bring you to the wedding site on an upper terrace above a little waterfall (on weekends you might have a little competition from a wedding party) or along an avenue of tree roses to a reflecting pool with cattails growing at either end.

Hundreds of roses are arranged in this formal garden, each one labeled so that if you can choose a favorite you can look for it at your nursery. Don't miss the tiny dwarf plants beneath the tree roses on the upper terrace. In late May or early June the roses will be freshly opened, but they continue to bloom well into October or November.

Because there are no tables here, this picnic is one that's easy to eat from a plate or tray in your lap. Benches are scattered throughout the garden and you can picnic on one of them, or spread out a ground cloth on a patch of grass or pine needles if you like the shade. Anywhere in the garden, a feeling of peace and order pervades the fragrant atmosphere.

Oakland Rose Garden Salade Niçoise Fare

SALADE NIÇOISE

COLD CURRIED RICE WITH CARROTS

CHEESE-FLAVORED CRACKERS

TEA WITH SODA

CARROT CAKE

SALAD NIÇOISE

8 lettuce leaves
1 cup lightly cooked
   green beans
One 6½-ounce can tuna
   fish, drained
4 anchovy fillets

8 black olives
½ green pepper, seeded
   and cut into strips
2 hard-boiled eggs,
   quartered

You'll need a separate container with a lid in which to compose each salad. The plastic trays that some frozen foods or fast foods come in are very good. Fasten them closed with rubber bands. On each tray, place 2 lettuce leaves. Arrange all the remaining ingredients, except the dressing, on the lettuce, and drizzle just a little French dressing (oil and vinegar type) over salad. Makes 4 salads.

COLD CURRIED RICE WITH CARROTS

2 teaspoons butter
2 tablespoons finely
   chopped green onions
1 teaspoon finely minced
   garlic
1 bay leaf

2 teaspoons curry powder
1 cup long-grain rice
1 small carrot, scraped and
   cut in thin strips or grated
1½ cups chicken broth

Melt the butter in a saucepan and add the green onions and garlic. Cook briefly, stirring, and add the bay leaf and curry powder. Add the rice and carrots, stirring. Add the broth and cover. Bring to a boil and let simmer for 20 minutes. Uncover and chill. Divide into 4 containers with lids to carry to the picnic. Serves 4.

TEA WITH SODA

To your favorite iced tea (a mix isn't bad this way) add equal amounts of sweet soda such as ginger ale.

CARROT CAKE

1½ cups all-purpose flour,
  sifted
1½ teaspoons baking
  powder
1 teaspoon baking soda
¼ teaspoon ground allspice
⅛ teaspoon ground nutmeg
1 teaspoon ground
  cinnamon
½ cup butter, softened
½ cup sugar

½ cup lightly packed brown
  sugar
2 eggs
1 teaspoon vanilla
1 teaspoon grated lemon
  rind
1½ cups grated peeled
  carrots
½ cup coarsely chopped
  nuts

Sift together the flour, baking powder, baking soda, and spices. Cream together the butter and sugar. Beat in the eggs. Add the flour mixture gradually. Add the vanilla, lemon rind, carrots, and nuts.

Bake in a buttered 9- by 5-inch loaf pan at 375°F. for 55 minutes. Let cool in pan. Wrap individual servings in plastic wrap. Whatever is left will keep well, or can be frozen. Makes 8 servings.

Packing Up

CHECK LIST B

Subtract the things on Check List A and the serving spoon.

COOLER

- ✓ containers of salad
- ✓ containers of rice
- ✓ cake, cut in servings and wrapped in plastic wrap

BASKET (or in the cooler if it will fit)

- ✓ utensils and glasses
- ✓ cheese crackers
- ✓ tea punch in plastic container
- ✓ optional coffee in a vacuum bottle

The garden is small enough so that you can leave the food in the car while you explore and then carry it to where you want to picnic. Once you've selected your rose-scented arbor, spread out your ground cloth or deploy the picnic things on a handy bench. Each person will have his own container, so only the drink and the cheese crackers will need to be passed. You can drowse here as long as you like amid the flowers, contented as a bee fresh from a blossom.

Picnics in the City

Palace of Fine Arts

41

From Marina Boulevard, in San Francisco, just west of the Marina Green, turn south on Baker Street. Restrooms, water. No tables, no barbecues. The entrance to the Exploratorium is on Lyon Street between Marina Boulevard and Richardson Avenue. Open Wednesday through Sunday from 1 to 5. Telephone (415) 563-7337. The theatre entrance is on Marina Boulevard and Lyon. Telephone (415) 563-6504.

One of the first things a newcomer to San Francisco must do is to get the palaces straight. The Palace of the Legion of Honor, a gift to the city from the Spreckels family in honor of the dead soldiers of World War I, is the one on top of the headlands in Lincoln Park. (Also a great place for a picnic.) The one we are heading for, the Palace of Fine Arts, is the romantic structure that you glimpse to your left as you follow 101 north to cross the Golden Gate Bridge. Designed by Bernard Maybeck as part of the Panama-Pacific Exposition in 1915, the palace was supposed to crumble away into a picturesque ruin, but safety precautions and a generous gift from Walter Johnson led to its restoration.

The small lawn by the lagoon is a delightful place to bring a brown bag lunch on a day that invites you outdoors. You'll be sharing the premises with the resident swans and the hundreds of canvasbacks, pintails, and mudhens that enjoy the small lake. You may want to bring a few bread crumbs for the swans and ducks, but beware! They can be very demanding if they sense a soft heart.

If you're not on your lunch hour, a picnic here can be combined with an hour or two of instructive fun in the Exploratorium, behind the main structure, where science is explained using all kinds of buttons and knobs to push and pull—a great place for experimenters of all ages.

Both palaces have theaters, and a preperformance picnic would be fun at either. But no other excuse is really needed than just a lovely day to be eating outdoors. Because it is hard to imagine a more romantic spot, this picnic is designed for two, so invite someone to share.

Palace of Fine Arts Deli Choice

YOUR SELECTIONS FROM THE
RECOMMENDATIONS BELOW

JAPANESE FOOD

If you like Japanese food, you can avoid any work in advance by stopping at the Ichi-Ban Kan restaurant in the Marina, 3347 Fillmore Street, for an obento box lunch. The food could include rice with sesame seeds, cold beef sukiyaki, kamaboko (a fish cake), chicken and vegetables in a wonton wrapper, or any number of other Oriental delicacies.

OTHER POSSIBILITIES

Some other good places in the city to pick up a picnic (though they are not close to the Palace of Fine Arts) are:

Acropolis Bakery and
  Delicatessen,
5217 Geary

Cafferata Ravioli Factory
700 Columbus

Casa Sanchez
2760 Twenty-fourth
  Street

Delices de France
320 Mason

Emporium's Market on
  Market
835 Market

Gloria Sausage Company
635 Vallejo

Herman's Delicatessen
Geary and Seventh
  Avenue

French Pantry
1570 California

Il Fornaio
2292 Union

Lucca Delicatessen
2120 Chestnut

Molinari
373 Columbus

Nancy Van Wyk Culinary
  Company
3548 Sacramento

New York City Deli
Market and Sixteenth

Oakville Grocery
1555 Pacific

Rodriguez Bakery
4499 Mission

Shenson's Jewish
  Delicatessen
5045 Geary

Speckmann's German
  restaurant and deli
1550 Church Street at
  Duncan

Yank Sing Tea House
671 Broadway

A SUPERMARKET PICNIC

For a picnic from the supermarket (the Marina Safeway is close to the Palace of Fine Arts and is reputedly a pretty romantic place itself) start with a small whole soft-ripened cheese such as a Camembert. (Brie tends to get out of control.) Choose another mild cheese for contrast, such as Gouda or Jarlsberg. In the bakery section, pick up a baguette to put the cheese on, and whatever looks irresistible for dessert. If you don't mind the fishy aroma, a can of small cross-packed sardines would be good. Otherwise, get a package of your choice of sliced meats.

Now, head for the produce counter and a few crispy vegetables and some fruit. Apples or pears would be good with the cheese, and strawberries are wonderfully romantic. If you don't have to work too hard in the afternoon, get a split of champagne. You'll need glasses, of course, which you can buy or bring along. If you don't want champagne, get a soft drink, bottles of fruit juice, or sparkling water. A package of napkins will finish up the shopping. You won't need plates, as the food can be attractively presented on a stack of napkins. Just be sure you have your pocket knife along to cut the bread and the cheese.

Do invite a significant other to share this picnic, because the Palace of Fine Arts provides a perfect setting for an escape back into the romantic era that produced this rococo treasure.

Oakland Museum 42

1000 Oak Street, Oakland. Open Wednesday through Saturday 10 to 5, Sunday, 12 to 7. Telephone (415) 273-3401. Some tables, restrooms, water. No barbecues.

Writer Alan Temko describes the Oakland Museum as "non-elitist," a characteristic that makes this marvelous building, designed to serve the people in a number of nonconventional ways, a great place for a picnic. The low, massive concrete walls give an almost eerie feeling of being in some ancient monument, and the garden court with its tiers of flowers spilling down the terraced ledges makes me feel that I've entered the

Hanging Gardens of Babylon. (Inside the museum is a painting of these fabled gardens, but it doesn't hold a candle to what's around you.) Even ubiquitous groups of touring schoolchildren can't destroy the feeling of tranquility inspired by the reflecting ponds, the sweep of the staircases, and the artfully placed sculpture.

If you come in from the Fallon Street side near Tenth Street, you can come right into the garden plaza without going through the building, and choose your spot to have lunch. You may find a table vacant, or you can sit on a parapet overlooking the gardens, or on the grass below.

Oakland Museum Ratto's Repast

YOUR SELECTIONS FROM THE
RECOMMENDATIONS BELOW

You don't even have to fix a lunch, because fairly close by are several places to buy some portable food.

ITALIAN FOOD

The best known is Ratto's Italian Delicatessen at 821 Washington Street, which has been there for more than ninety years. Besides the delicatessen food, open bins and jars hold an incredible selection of various grains, including polenta and mandioca, and there are various types of pastas, breads, and cooking utensils. You can even buy a basket to carry your picnic in. Cook's Champagne, which I find very good for a modest price, is one of hundreds of wines available. If you choose a sandwich, condiments are stored on a handy nearby shelf for you to doctor up your own. I'd recommend some marinated mushrooms, too.

CHINESE FOOD

Closer to the museum, and equally fascinating, are two Chinese grocery-deli-restaurants. New Sand Choung Market at 377 Eighth Street is closest, and Kwong Far Company at 940 Webster is about five blocks away. At either of these places you can get barbecued pork, chow mein, egg rolls, and various other specialties. I must confess I'm not adventurous enough to try duck's feet or boiled pork stomach, but you might want to experiment with some such less-conventional tidbits.

Any of these places is fascinating to browse in, so if you're on your lunch break, don't get distracted. When you've chosen your picnic, walk over to the museum and enjoy lunching in the Hanging Gardens of Oakland.

Embarcadero Center   43

Between Sacramento and Clay from the waterfront at Drumm to Battery, San Francisco.

The Embarcadero Center offers not only several places to enjoy eating your workday lunch outdoors, but also provides places to buy all the essentials. Even if you don't work in the area, it's easy to get there on BART, a cable car, or a bus. You can, of course, save some time, energy, and money by bringing a lunch from home like the one described below, but if you don't, here are some of the places to find food to eat outside.

In Building One (farthest from the water) on the street level are Eppler's Bakery with breads and pastries, Hong Kong Express for Chinese deli food, and Norm's Sandwich Shop where you can eat your sandwich at an outside table. Building Two has McDonald's on the lobby level (second floor) for people who feel they deserve a break, and Building Three has Just Desserts, and Mrs. Robinson's with gourmet food and wines on the lobby level. You can call ahead here at 398-0180 and your take-out lunch will be ready for you. Sprouts, on the street level, is for natural-food fanciers, and has take-out service.

Now, for places to eat. When you enter the complex through Embarcadero Three on the Drumm Street side, go up the escalator and make your way along the open walkways that link the buildings. You can stop right there, if you like, and enjoy your food at one of the tables provided.

If you keep going, you'll come to a three-story stainless steel sculpture that looks like child's whistle. Bear right and take the walkway across toward the townhouses. Between the Alcoa Building and a bar called the Punch Line, is a small raised garden with a ledge all around it, which provides a comfortable spot for a picnic.

Four similar places are found at the four corners of the Alcoa Buiding. Each has a small enclosed square with grass on the raised center area, and, on the grass, a sculpture that will give you something to contemplate while you munch. The standing figure is *Knife Edge*, by Henry Moore, and the geometric figure is *Iconsaspirale*, by Charles Perry; *Limits of Horizon One*, by Jack Peter Stern, fills another corner and *Horse*, by Mario Marini, the fourth. You can find either sun or shade in these charming pocket parks.

Across Maritime Plaza, bounded by Jackson and Pacific and Front and Drumm streets, is Walton Park, a tree-shaded green area that is suprisingly quiet in view of all the surrounding freeway traffic. It's a little like being inside a moving sculpture!

If you do want to bring a lunch from home, try this brown-bag special for one that calls for a little advance thought, but very little work.

Embarcadero Buy-It or Bring-It Lunch

CHICKEN BROILED WITH MUSTARD

MARINATED GREEN BEANS

SMALL CARTON OF YOGURT

GRAHAM CRACKERS SPREAD WITH CREAM CHEESE

COFFEE OR FRUIT JUICE

CHICKEN BROILED WITH MUSTARD

Cook the chicken and green beans and eat them hot for dinner the night before; the leftovers will be equally delicious cold the next day.

1 frying chicken, cut into parts	4 tablespoons butter, melted
	2 teaspoons dry mustard
Salt and pepper to taste	1 tablespoon water

Sprinkle the chicken pieces with the salt and pepper. Place skin side down on a broiler rack. Brush with 2 tablespoons of

the butter. Broil for 10 minutes. Turn and brush with the remaining butter. Cook until done, watching carefully.
Chicken is done when juices from the thickest part of the
thigh run clear when it is pricked.

Dissolve the dry mustard in the water and baste the
chicken with it. Broil another minute, just until bubbly.
Serves 2 with some for leftovers.

MARINATED GREEN BEANS

1 pound fresh green beans
2 tablespoons French
    dressing (oil and vinegar
    type), with garlic and
    herbs

Cook the beans in a large kettle of boiling water until just
tender. To eat them hot, drain and butter. To use them for
next day, put a serving in a container with a lid. Add the
French dressing and let them marinate until lunchtime.
Serves 2 with some left over for the picnic.

No packing-up directions are needed here; I'm sure you can
get a lunch into a sack without help. Just don't forget a spoon
for the yogurt.

In spite of its size and complexity, Embarcadero Center has
a feeling of intimacy and informality that makes taking out
your brown bag lunch in one of its sunny corners a cheering
and pleasurable event.

Emeryville
Marina

44

---

*From Highway 17 in Emeryville, take the Powell Street exit
west to the end. Tables, barbecues, restrooms, water.*

When you drive out past the apartments and restau-
rants to the very end of this man-made spit of land,
you'll find the marina enclosed on one side, and a
grassy, landscaped area on the Bay side with tables
overlooking the Bay Bridge and San Francisco. With
the Bay sparkling in the foreground and Mount Tam
lifting its unmistakable profile north of the city, it's
hard to believe you're so close to downtown Oakland.

On a windy day, you might like the more sheltered tables on the side of the spit near the boats, where you'll even find a fire pit.

Though smaller than the Berkeley Marina with its adjacent park and restaurants, the Emeryville location offers much better picnicking. At Berkeley, the only tables are in Shorebird Park. Though tables are not a necessity of life, the Berkeley Marina also has a very limited view back toward Alameda, since the Bay side is taken up with parking and the fishing pier. You can picnic on benches or on the grass facing the boat harbor at Berkeley, but the Emeryville Marina offers better views with greater comfort. Another plus here is the access under Powell Street to the mudflats, for a close look at the famous woodscrap sculptures on your way to or fro. You can hike or bicycle here, or fish from the small pier if your time is your own.

On your lunch hour, you won't want to have the picnic suggested here (see Picnics 9, 21, 27, 37, or 43 for lunchtime ideas) but if after work or on a holiday, this menu makes a marvelous supper.

Emeryville Marina Mixed Seafood Grill

PEA SOUP WITH MINT

MIXED SEAFOOD GRILL

HARD ROLLS

CHERRY TOMATOES

APPLESAUCE CAKE

CHABLIS

COFFEE

PEA SOUP WITH MINT

2 tablespoons butter
1 tablespoon chopped onion
2 cups fresh or frozen green peas
½ teaspoon sugar

2 cups chicken broth
1 cup milk or cream
1 tablespoon chopped fresh mint
Salt to taste

Melt the butter in a pot, add the onion and cook, stirring, until the onion is translucent. Add the peas, sugar, and broth and cook until the peas are tender. Purée in a blender or processor. Return to the pot, add the milk or cream and mint, and taste for salt.

This soup can be served hot or cold, depending on the weather. Carry to the picnic in a wide-mouthed vacuum bottle. Serves 4.

MIXED SEAFOOD GRILL

4 fish fillets (sea bass, flounder, or sole), about 4 ounces each	1 green pepper, seeded and cut into strips
½ pound raw shrimp	Butter
½ pound boned chicken thigh meat	4 thin lemon slices
8 large mushrooms	2 tablespoons sake or sherry
	Soy sauce

Sprinkle the fish with salt. Shell and devein the shrimp, leaving the tails intact. Blanch the shrimp for 10 seconds in boiling salted water, drain, and cool. Cut the chicken into 1-inch cubes and score lightly to ensure quick cooking. Wipe the mushrooms with a damp towel and cut them lengthwise into ¼-inch slices.

Butter the centers of four 12-inch squares of aluminum foil. In the center of each square, place a fish fillet, skin side up. On top and around it arrange the shrimp, chicken, mushroom slices, and green pepper strips. Top with a pat of butter and a lemon slice. Sprinkle about ½ tablespoon sake or sherry over each portion. Fold up into a packet and crimp the edges so that the packet is tightly sealed. Refrigerate until picnic time.

At the picnic, place the packets on a grill above hot coals and grill for 10 minutes. Do not turn. To serve, place the packets on plates and let the diners open them. Pass some soy sauce. Serves 4.

APPLESAUCE CAKE

This cake travels well and keeps well.

½ cup shortening or butter	¼ teaspoon salt
1½ cups sugar	1 teaspoon baking powder
2 eggs, beaten	½ teaspoon baking soda
1 cup unsweetened thick applesauce	1 teaspoon ground cinnamon
2 cups all-purpose unsifted flour	½ teaspoon ground cloves
	1 cup raisins

Thoroughly cream the shortening or butter and sugar. Add the eggs and beat well. Add the applesauce. Sift the dry ingredients together and add to the batter. Beat smooth and fold in the raisins.

Bake in a well-greased 8-inch square pan at 350°F. for 45 to 60 minutes, or until a tester inserted in the center comes out clean. Makes 6 servings.

Packing Up

TO CHECK LIST C, ADD:

🗸 cups or mugs for soup

COOLER

🗸 seafood packets
🗸 cherry tomatoes in a rigid container

🗸 butter for rolls
🗸 wine

BASKET

🗸 vacuum bottle of soup
🗸 vacuum bottle of coffee
🗸 soy sauce
🗸 rolls wrapped in aluminum foil for heating

🗸 cake wrapped in plastic wrap
🗸 plates and utensils

EXTRA CONTAINER

🗸 the charcoal and other barbecue gear

When you've selected your table on either the Bay side or marina side, get the charcoal started, and then serve the soup while you wait for the coals to burn down nicely. Put the packets of fish and meats on the grill, and when they are done, serve each person one. Pass the soy sauce, the rolls and butter, and the cherry tomatoes. Being so close to the bright blue water under (I hope) a bright blue sky should give everyone a healthy appetite for this elegant grill.

Overfelt Gardens

45

In San Jose between Highways 680 and 101 on McKee Road at Educational Park Drive. Open from 10:00 A.M. to sunset daily. Telephone (408) 251-3323. Tables, restrooms, water.

In the midst of the housing developments, small bus-inesses, and shopping centers that make up this section of San Jose is an oasis of calm and beauty: thirty-three acres of garden that were originally part of

Several quick-food places along McKee Road pro-vide take-out food to be consumed in the peace and quiet of the garden. If it seems somewhat sacrilegious, you can bring a brown bag lunch from home.

home to the city of San Jose for a special community park. Her park was to have no playgrounds or ball-fields; it was to be a place designed to provide peace and solitude in the midst of the city bustle. And so it does.

Three ponds in the garden provide habitat for migra-tory birds and other wildlife, and the surrounding areas have been planted with flowers and grasses. One of the ponds reflects a thirty-foot bronze and marble statue of Confucius, a gift from the people of Taiwan. A most imposing Chinese arch leads to this pleasant grassy area.

As you stroll through the garden, you can take an arboreal walk, identifying trees by their numbers. (The collection of palms is particularly interesting.) A fragrance garden will provide a treat for your nose.

When you're ready for lunch, the picnic tables are located near McKee Road. The main entrance to the garden is on Educational Drive, but you can park on McKee Road and walk in through the south gate to be right at the tables. They are well shaded and in a pleasant, grassy lawn area. The only drawback to Miss Overfelt's original intention is the traffic noise from the street. To avoid this, you can do without a table and spread out a mat or jacket farther away from the street and enjoy your picnic near one of the ponds. If a party of schoolchildren comes whooping through, just be patient. They'll soon be off to another part of the garden.

Several quick-food places along McKee Road provide take-out food to be consumed in the peace and quiet of the garden. If it seems somewhat sacrilegious, you can bring a brown bag lunch from home.

Near the garden are a Taco Charley's, a Sambo's, and a McDonald's. A Chinese food restaurant on nearby Jackson Avenue can also provide take-out food. Across the street from the garden and a few blocks west is a fruit and vegetable stand that can help you round out the picnic with something healthful and tasty. I'd vote for tacos, myself, because I'm so fond of them that I like almost any version.

Overfelt Gardens Junk Food Junket

TACO CHARLEYS' TACOS

SOFT DRINKS

TWO FRESH VEGETABLES

FRESH FRUIT

Packing Up

TO BUY ON THE WAY

✔ all menu items

When you've collected your lunch and picked out the prettiest place in the garden, wash the vegetables and fruit and enjoy it all. I think Miss Overfelt would forgive us our junk food if she knew how much it means to picnic lovers to have such a lovely place to consume it.

Picnics by Lakes & Streams

Hogback Island County Park

46

From Highway 160 north of Isleton, take Poverty Road north to a T intersection at Walker Landing Road. Turn left and continue until you come up on the levee. The park is to the left, at the intersection with Grand Island Road. Tables, barbecues, restrooms. No water. Free.

Undeniably the best place to picnic in the Sacra-mento–San Joaquin Delta is on a boat. Cruising the pleasant waterways to fish or water-ski, you can find an endless number of spots to anchor and to enjoy a meal from the galley. If you don't have a boat yourself, but know someone who does, maybe you could offer to bring the picnic.

But what about us landlubbers without boat-owning friends? Most Delta roads follow levees and are narrow, with steep banks on either side, so that it's impossible to park and just enjoy the river. Most of the tempting places have been usurped by private mari-nas. (If you see one you especially like, stop and ask the fee for picnicking. It will probably be minimal.) But there are a few public parks that provide safe parking and wonderful picnicking. My favorite is Hog-back Island just north of Isleton. This relatively small county park is on a tree-shaded island with blackberry vines growing profusely near the water. If you are here in July or August you may be able to supplement the picnic with some fresh berries.

The island is shaped like a ship with its prow head-ing into Steamboat Slough, and if you choose a table out at the tip, the water laps on both sides of you and you really feel as if you're on a boat.

After the picnic, if you'd like a real, though brief, boat ride, you can continue north on Grand Island Road, following the signs to the ferry. A tiny car-ferry will transport you across to Ryer Island. Go three miles across the island, turn left, and in five more miles you'll come to a second boat that will take you across to a road leading south to Rio Vista. These free ferry rides are an experience everyone should try at least once. (They'll also take you if you're on a bike.)

If swimming is your chief interest in coming to the Park on Highway 160 about thirteen miles north of the Antioch Bridge. The picnic area there is near the beach on Seven Mile Slough. You'll find barbecues, restrooms, and lots of tables, many of them in the shade. Like other state parks, the fee is two dollars for day use. Brannan Island is also famous for its burrowing owls; they're hard to see, but you might get lucky.

For people who like to watch river traffic, Sandy Beach County Park just south of Rio Vista is located where you can see the main river channel and keep your eye on a drawbridge which may open to let a big ship come through. A whistle will alert you and the bridge keeper. This beach is indeed sandy, and on a windy day a picnic tends to get rather crunchy. Shade is provided by plastic sunscreens, and there are barbecues, tables, and restrooms. Day use is one dollar when someone is there to collect.

Even though the boating, swimming, and fishing are wonderful in summer, try the Delta sometime on a clear winter or spring day when the countryside is green and sparkling and you can see for miles all the way to the Sierras in the east, and to Mount Diablo towering over the western outlook. The main-dish soup for this picnic is equally good hot or cold, depending on your choice of seasons.

Delta Vichyssoise Delectation

MELON OR FIGS WITH PROSCIUTTO

VICHYSSOISE

CUCUMBER SALAD

RED AND GREEN PEPPER STRIPS

BREAD STICKS

CHABLIS

LEMON TARTS

COFFEE

MELON OR FIGS WITH PROSCIUTTO

Cut a melon into serving slices, or peel 4 figs. Wrap a slice of prosciutto around the fruit, fastening with a toothpick. If you're using figs, sprinkle them with a pinch of chopped fresh mint for garnish. Serves 4.

VICHYSSOISE

If the weather is cold, serve this hot and call it potato soup.

2 cups peeled and sliced
   potatoes
2 cups sliced onions
4 cups chicken broth
1 cup milk or cream

1 teaspoon salt
2 tablespoons chopped fresh
   chives or green onion tops
   for garnish

Simmer the potatoes and onions in the chicken broth until tender. Purée in a blender or food processor. Add the milk. If serving hot, heat almost to boiling, then put in a wide-mouthed vacuum bottle. If serving cold, chill thoroughly. Add the salt. Bring the chives or onion tops separately to garnish soup before serving. Serves 4.

LEMON TARTS

4 individual tart shells,
   baked about 5 minutes
3 eggs
½ cup sugar
Grated zest and juice of 2
   lemons

After the tart shells have baked at 400°F. for 5 minutes, turn the oven down to 375°F. and remove the shells to cool slightly. Mix together the eggs, sugar, lemon zest, and lemon juice until thoroughly blended.

Pour the filling into the tart shells and bake until the centers are set and the tops are slightly golden, about 15 to 20 minutes. When the tarts are cool, wrap them, still in the pans, in plastic wrap for transporting to the picnic. Makes 4 servings.

Packing Up

TO CHECK LIST B, ADD:

✔ bowls or mugs for the
   soup
✔ soup spoons

COOLER

- fruit with prosciutto in a plastic container
- cucumber salad in a plastic container
- pepper strips in a plastic bag
- wine
- bottle of water

BASKET

- vacuum bottle of soup
- vacuum bottle of coffee
- bread sticks
- lemon tarts, wrapped in pans
- plates and utensils

When the table is selected and set, give people the first course of fruit with prosciutto. Then open the wine and serve the soup. Pass the bread sticks, the salad, and the pepper slices. The coffee and lemon tarts will round out your peaceful picnic at the river's edge.

San Mateo County Memorial Park

47

From Highway 84 just south of La Honda, take Pescadero Road south. Telephone (415) 879-0212. Tables, barbecues, restrooms, water.

Philosophies of what a park should be have changed over the passing years. The current trend is to value most the preservation of wilderness: to interfere as little as possible with what nature has provided. Earlier parks were often planned for the maximum comfort and pleasure of the visitors. One such park is San Mateo County Memorial. Established in 1924 to honor the veterans of World War I, it has the civilized, orderly air of an earlier time when population pressures were fewer and it was still considered possible to improve upon nature.

The deep, deep shade of the virgin redwoods with cathedral-like aisles between them, the dammed-up creek where you can swim in summer, the camp store, and the naturalist programs all make Memorial a comfortable as well as beautiful park. These things also make it popular, so plan to arrive early.

On crowded weekends, you may want to go on past and try Pescadero Creek Park, Wunderlich, or Sam McDonald (see Picnic 37), all lovely wilderness parks in the new style, and less used than the more accessible older park.

But I hope you will find a place along Pescadero Creek at Memorial. The softly running water, the deeply dappled shade among the giant tree trunks, the harsh quarreling of the Stellar Jays as they keep a tamed eye on the picnic sites, all add to the feeling of being at home in your own private giant backyard. One of the amenities of Memorial is that you can drive your car right to the picnic sites, so it's no trouble to bring along everything needed for a traditional barbecue in this traditional park.

San Mateo Steak Barbecue

MELON CUBES IN PORT

MARINATED SIRLOIN STEAK

SWEET-POTATO SALAD

TOMATO, MUSHROOM, AVOCADO, AND
ENDIVE SALAD

ROLLS & BUTTER

CABERNET SAUVIGNON OR ZINFANDEL

LOAF CAKE OR WATERMELON

COFFEE

MARINATED SIRLOIN STEAK

One 2-pound sirloin, flank,
  or porterhouse steak
¾ cup red wine
¼ cup oil
1 small onion, chopped

1 clove garlic, pressed
½ teaspoon dried oregano
1 teaspoon salt
1 bay leaf

Place steak in a container just large enough to accommodate it. Combine the wine, oil, onion, and seasonings and marinate steak for 2 hours at room temperature or overnight in the refrigerator.

At the picnic, barbecue the steak for about 5 minutes on each side, about 2 inches from the coals. Check for doneness by cutting a small slit in a thick spot. When done to your taste, slice across grain in thin slices to serve. Serves 4.

SWEET-POTATO SALAD

1 pound sweet potatoes
1 cup thinly sliced celery
½ cup thinly sliced green onions
1 large red apple, diced
½ cup mayonnaise
1 teaspoon prepared mustard
1 teaspoon grated orange peel
1 tablespoon orange juice
2 tablespoons finely chopped crystallized ginger
Salt and pepper to taste

Cook the sweet potatoes in boiling water to cover until tender when pierced, about 30 minutes. Do not cook until mushy. Drain; cool, peel, and cut into ½-inch cubes. Combine the sweet potatoes, celery, onions, and apple.

Stir together all the remaining ingredients except the salt and pepper and pour this dressing over the potato mixture and mix well. Season to taste with salt and pepper. Chill. Place in a plastic container with a lid to carry to picnic. Serves 4.

TOMATO, MUSHROOM, AVOCADO, AND ENDIVE SALAD

1 avocado, peeled, pitted, and cubed
Dressing, following
1 Belgian endive, cut into lengthwise shreds
¼ pound mushrooms, sliced
½ pint cherry tomatoes, stemmed
4 lettuce leaves

Gently toss the avocado with some of the following dressing. Carry the endive, mushrooms, tomatoes, dressing, and lettuce leaves to the picnic in separate containers or self-sealing plastic bags.

At the picnic, arrange the vegetables on the lettuce leaves, and drizzle the dressing over them. Serves 4.

Dressing

2 tablespoons wine vinegar
1 tablespoon prepared French mustard
Salt and pepper to taste
Scant ½ cup salad or olive oil

In a small bowl combine all the ingredients except the oil. Add oil gradually in a small stream, whisking until well combined.

Packing Up

CHECK LIST C

Bring a carving knife and fork for the steak, and be sure your cutting board is adequate. Do bring a tablecloth for this one!

COOLER

- melon in port in a container with lid
- steak in a closed container
- sweet-potato salad in container with a lid
- ingredients for tomato salad in self-sealing plastic bags
- salad dressing in a tightly closed jar
- butter for the rolls wrapped in plastic

BASKET

- rolls in a sack
- wine
- vacuum bottle of coffee
- plates and utensils
- tablecloth

SEPARATE CONTAINER

- the charcoal and starter
- other grilling equipment

If you're bringing a watermelon, you need a separate small cooler for that. If you're bringing cake, it can go in the basket.

Your first job will be to start the coals for the steak. Then you can set the table and serve everyone some of the melon that has been soaking in port. When the coals are burned down well, cook the steak and slice it thinly across the grain. It can be served on the cutting board. Compose the green salad, and pass that along with the sweet-potato salad and rolls. The wine can be opened to breathe a little when you start the steak.

The jays and maybe some other picnickers, too, will no doubt admire the luscious smells wafting up from your picnic fire under the ancient redwood trees. To be fair, we should drink one toast to the Doughboys of 1917–18, who would no doubt be pleased with their memorial park.

Russian River Canoe Trip

48

From San Francisco, take Highway 101 north. Watch for the Healdsburg exit and Russian River resort area signs.

If you've never tried canoeing, the shallow and rela-tively quiet-flowing Russian River makes a great place to start. When we first rented our aluminum canoe, we wondered why the poor thing looked so battered, but we soon found out. Inexperienced canoers like ourselves had dragged it over low water, crashed it into the bank, and scraped it over rocks and tree trunks just as we did. We also turned over during the first fifteen minutes, which reduced the anxiety about how to handle that. It's fairly simple: the mandatory life jacket holds you up, you drag the canoe to shore, empty out the water, and replace your now sodden belongings in the bottom. Anything that you don't want to get wet—and that certainly includes the lunch—belongs in a waterproof bag, tied securely to the canoe. With self-sealing plastic bags, your food can stay dry and appetizing for a picnic on one of the many sandy beaches along the river, even if you get rather soggy yourself. Your appetite should really be good after all that paddling! This picnic is designed for two people, since that's all the usual canoe will hold. Bring the amount of food you need, and freeze what is left for another outing.

Keep your center of gravity low and your lunch dry, and remember the sunscreen, a hat, drinking water, and a rope to tie everything securely to the canoe. You don't want to carry anything extra on this trip, so everything in this menu can be eaten with the fingers, straight from the container. You won't even need napkins, since you can wash your fingers off in the river.

Several firms along the Russian River rent canoes for day trips. Try one of these:

W. C. Trowbridge
  Canoe Trips
13849 Old Redwood
  Highway,
Healdsburg CA 95448
Telephone (707) 857-3872

Canoe Trips West
2170 Redwood Highway
Greenbrae, CA 94901
Telephone (415) 461-1750
  (for day trips or longer)

California Rivers
21001 Geyserville Avenue
Geyserville, CA 95441
Telephone (707) 857-3872

Russian River Waterproof Cheeseburger pie

CHEESEBURGER PIE

PACKAGES OF CORN CHIPS

SLICED RAW BROCCOLI, ZUCCHINI, MUSHROOMS

APPLES OR ORANGES

BEER & WATER

MOLASSES CAKE

CHEESEBURGER PIE

1 pound ground beef
1½ cups chopped onion
½ teaspoon salt
¼ teaspoon pepper
1 cup shredded Cheddar
  cheese (about 4 ounces)

1½ cups milk
¾ cup biscuit mix
3 eggs

Lightly grease a large pie tin. Cook the ground beef and onion in a frying pan until the beef is brown; drain. Stir in the salt and pepper. Spread in the pie tin and sprinkle with the cheese. Beat the remaining ingredients together until smooth. Pour into the pie tin.

Bake at 400°F. until the pie is golden brown and a knife inserted in the center comes out clean. Cool. Cut into serving pieces. Extra servings will keep in refrigerator or can be frozen. Wrap each serving in plastic wrap, then place in a self-sealing plastic bag. Makes 6 to 8 servings.

MOLASSES CAKE

1½ cups butter, softened	1½ teaspoons ground ginger
1½ cups firmly packed dark brown sugar	½ teaspoon ground mace
4 eggs	½ teaspoon ground cloves
4½ cups all-purpose flour	1½ teaspoons baking soda
1½ teaspoons ground cinnamon	1½ cups unsulfured molasses
	1½ cups milk

Cream together the butter and sugar until light and fluffy. Beat in the eggs, one at a time. Sift together the flour and spices. Add the baking soda to the molasses. Add the dry ingredients, the molasses, and the milk alternately to the batter, about a third of each at a time, and mix well.

Pour into a buttered 13- by 9- inch baking pan, and bake at 350°F. for 50 to 60 minutes, or until a tester comes out clean. Cool on a rack. Cut into squares. Wrap servings in plastic wrap, and place in a self-sealing plastic bag. Makes 6 servings.

Packing Up

All the food and drink can go in a cooler with a handle. If you want to bring a lot of beer, you may need a separate cooler for that. Tie a rope around the cooler so the lid will stay on, then tie the rope to the canoe. Wrap all the food securely in plastic wrap, then place it in self-sealing bags. If you're not concerned about having the food stay cold (it need not for safety's sake) it can simply be placed in a waterproof sack and tied in the canoe. The picnic will stay dry and appetizing, no matter how wet and bedraggled the picnickers may be!

Vasona Lake County Park   49

North of Highway 17 in Los Gatos between Blossom Hill Road and Lark Avenue. Take the Lark Avenue exit from Highway 17, go north to University, turn left (west), and go along the top edge of the park to Blossom Hill Road. Turn left (south) and pass Oak Meadow Park, then turn left into Vasona Lake Park. Tables, barbecues, restrooms, water. No swimming.

Vasona Lake Park is one of those urban parks with a freeway along one side and busy streets along another that still gives you the feeling of being in the country. For water lovers, it has both a lake and a creek, so you can choose your favorite ambience.

The city of Los Gatos runs the small Oak Meadow Park that is adjacent to Vasona Lake along Blossom Hill Road. Pass the entrance to this park, cross the creek, and turn into the County Park. The picnic places I like best are near the boat-launching area, but drive around the park a little and pick you own favorite spot. Once you've parked, you can walk around the lake or along the creek, then come back to your car for the food for the picnic.

A boat-rental concession rents canoes, rowboats, or sailboats by the hour. You can launch your own boat here once you get permission.

For a creekside setting, follow the creek toward Oak Meadow Park and choose whatever spot you like. In this direction you'll come to the railroad station where a miniature train operates Saturday from 11, Sunday from noon, to 5:37 (!) on both days.

In spite of all the activities offered, the lake maintains a peaceful calm, and seems to have the same effect on the people who come to enjoy the scene. Here is a peaceful picnic that's easy to prepare ahead.

Vasona Lake Peaceful Chicken Feed

COLD CHICKEN VINAIGRETTE

BROCCOLI SALAD

FRENCH BREAD

CHERRY TOMATOES

BLANC DE BLANCS

SYLLABUB

COFFEE

COLD CHICKEN VINAIGRETTE

4 whole chicken breasts, halved
4 cups water
½ onion
1 carrot, sliced
1 stalk celery, sliced
1 bay leaf
6 peppercorns
2 teaspoons salt
Vinaigrette Sauce, following

Put the chicken breasts in the water and add the remaining ingredients. Cover the pot and bring to boil. Skim off the foam, replace the cover, lower the heat, and simmer until fork tender, about 10 to 12 minutes. Remove, cool, skin, and bone the breasts. Spoon the following sauce over the chicken just before serving. Serves 4.

Vinaigrette Sauce

2 tablespoons wine vinegar
⅛ teaspoon salt
¼ teaspoon dry mustard
6 tablespoons oil
Pinch of pepper
1 teaspoon chopped capers
1 teaspoon finely minced green onions
2 tablespoons minced fresh parsley

Put the vinegar, salt, mustard, oil, and pepper in a screw-top jar and shake vigorously. Add the remaining ingredients and shake again. Shake once more before pouring over chicken.

SYLLABUB

¾ cup superfine granulated sugar
½ cup Madeira
¼ cup cognac
Grated rind and juice of 2 lemons
2 cups heavy cream

Whisk together all the ingredients except the cream, beating until the sugar is dissolved. In another bowl, whip the cream until it holds soft peaks. Pour in the sugar mixture in a stream while beating, and continue to beat until thick. Pour the syllabub into 4 individual containers (plastic glasses work well) and chill. Put plastic wrap over the top and fasten with a rubber band. Carry to the picnic in cooler, making sure the glasses stay upright. Serves 4.

Packing Up

CHECK LIST B

COOLER

- chicken breasts, in a large container with a lid
- vinaigrette sauce in a container with a tight lid
- broccoli salad, in a plastic container with a lid
- cherry tomatoes in a self-sealing plastic bag
- wine
- syllabub in individual containers

BASKET

- bread
- vacuum bottle of coffee
- plates and utensils

After a pleasant stroll along the lake or the creek, take out the picnic. Pour the vinaigrette sauce on the chicken and stir gently. Serve each person. Pass the salad, bread, and tomatoes and pour everyone a glass of wine. This is a light but delightful lunch, and the syllabub should top it off perfectly, leaving everyone ready for a nap along the lakeshore.

Dimond Park · 50

From Highway 580 in Oakland, exit east on Fruitvale and go five blocks to Lyman for the entrance to the park. Restrooms, water.

On a map of Oakland, Dimond Canyon is a long, green, skinny line that begins at Fruitvale Avenue and winds up to Redwood Regional Park. An intrepid hiker can follow it all the way to the string of regional parks that top the Oakland Hills along Skyline Boulevard, but the picnicker who just wants a peaceful, sylvan spot beside a stream in the middle of Oakland need not go so far.

Start at Dimond Park with its charmingly landscaped tree-shaded lawn area, complete with an outdoor swimming pool, tennis courts, and children's play areas. Walk toward the pool, passing Dimond

Cottage, built from handmade adobe bricks in 1897 as a playhouse for the children of the original owner of these grounds. Across the lawn from the swimming pool, you'll find Sausal Creek. Follow it to El Centro, then cross the road and go through the stile to begin your stroll along the delightful shaded creekside.

Here, just a few hundred yards from a busy street, you'll hear only the gurgle of the softly flowing stream wending its way through redwoods and bay trees. Blackberries are abundant, and if they're in season you may want to pick a few to add to the picnic, but do be sure that the vines you are tramping through are not the ubiquitous poison oak.

Back in the thirties, the WPA lined the creek with concrete, but it is now worn and moss-covered, and the effect is so bucolic that when the Leimert Bridge looms overhead, it seems an impossible intrusion. Past here, the path is rougher, and you can turn back to find a spot to dangle your feet over the stream while you picnic. It's a good idea to bring something to sit on, even if it's just your windbreaker, as the ground tends to be damp. This picnic is easy to carry, either in a paper bag or your day pack.

Dimond Park Chicken Delight

CHICKEN ROLLS WITH SPINACH AND FETA CHEESE

BUTTERED HARD ROLLS

ASSORTED VEGETABLES

FRESH FRUIT

BROWNIES

GREY RIESLING

COFFEE, WATER

CHICKEN ROLLS WITH SPINACH AND FETA CHEESE

This recipe is not as much trouble as it looks, especially if you have a good sharp knife to bone the chicken. The results are well worth the effort!

3 tablespoons butter
1 clove garlic, minced
½ teaspoon dried rosemary
½ cup chopped cooked
  spinach, well drained
¼ cup grated feta cheese
1½ tablespoons bread
  crumbs

1 egg yolk
¼ teaspoon pepper
2 whole chicken breasts,
  halved, skinned, and
  boned

Melt the butter in a small skillet and cook the garlic and rosemary briefly. Combine the spinach and feta in a mixing bowl. Pour the butter mixture over the spinach; mix thoroughly. Stir in the bread crumbs, egg yolk, and pepper. Set aside.

Using a mallet or rolling pin, pound or roll the breasts out flat, about ¼ inch thick. Using about ¼ cup for each piece, divide the filling among the chicken breasts, making a cylindrical shape down the center of each. Roll each chicken breast into a cylinder to enclose the filling and secure with a toothpick.

Add water to a steamer to 1 inch below the rack and bring it to full boil. Place the chicken rolls on the rack, cover, and steam for 15 minutes. Cool, then wrap in plastic wrap. If you don't have a steamer, use a colander or a rack set on a tuna can with both ends removed. Serves 4.

BROWNIES

2 eggs
1 cup sugar
1 teaspoon vanilla
Two 1-ounce squares
  unsweetened baking
  chocolate

½ cup butter
½ cup sifted all-purpose
  flour
⅛ teaspoon salt
1 cup coarsely chopped
  walnuts

Beat the eggs until thick and lemon colored. Add the sugar, beating until the mixture is fluffy. Stir in the vanilla, and the chocolate melted carefully with the butter. Fold in the flour, salt, and ¾ cup of the walnuts.

Pour into a greased 9-inch square metal baking pan. Sprinkle with the remaining walnuts. Bake at 350°F. for 20 minutes. Cool in the pan and cut into squares. Wrap at least 2 apiece in plastic wrap. Makes 12.

Packing Up

At home, divide the portions among four sacks. They can be put in a day pack for easy carrying. If you are bringing wine, one person will need to carry that, another the glasses. All the foods can be carried in self-sealing plastic sacks. Bring a corkscrew and napkins.

I do believe I saved the best for last. There's something about finding a serene, wooded spot like this in the heart of a city that is like knowing a secret. And the chicken rolls and brownies are really good, too! All that's needed is a few hours of time and some special friends to share them with.

Bibliography

Doss, Margot Patterson. *San Francisco at Your Feet.* Rev. ed. New York: Grove Press, 1974.

Johnston, Joanne. *J.J.'s Best Bike Trips.* Berkeley: Ten Speed Press, 1972.

Levine, Beverly. *Picked This Morning.* San Francisco: Chronicle Books, 1980.

Milne, Terry. *The Ultimate Bay Book.* San Francisco: California Living Books, 1979.

Pomada, Elizabeth. *Places to Go with Children.* Rev. ed. San Francisco: Chronicle Books, 1976.

Rennert, Amy. *Where Can We Go This Weekend?* Los Angeles: J. P. Tarcher, 1980.

Sunset Books. *California Wine Country.* Menlo Park, Calif.: Lane Publishing Company, 1980.

Taber, Tom. *Discovering San Francisco Bay.* San Mateo, Calif.: Oak Valley Press, 1978.

Geographical List of Picnic Spots

Alameda County
Coyote Hills Regional Park, 12
Dimond Park, 174–175
Emeryville Marina, 154–155
Joaquin Miller Regional Park
    and Woodminster
    Amphitheatre, 66–67
Morcom Amphitheatre of
    Roses, 143
Oakland Museum, 150–151
Point Pinole Regional
    Shoreline Park, 45–46
Robert W. Crown Memorial
    State Beach, 39
Sunol Regional Wilderness
    Park, 56–57
U.C. Botanical Gardens,
    135–136

Contra Costa County
Black Diamond Mines
    Regional Preserve, 84–85
Concord Pavilion, 63–64
Contra Loma Regional Park,
    114–115
John Muir Home National
    Historic Site, 82–83
Morgan Territory Regional
    Preserve, 132
Mount Diablo State Park,
    20–21

Marin County
Audubon Canyon Ranch,
    48–49
China Camp State Park,
    91–92
Marin Headlands, 9–10
Mount Tamalpais Mountain
    Theatre, 69–70
Tomales Bay State Park, 117

Napa County
Cuvaison Winery, 107
Robert Louis Stevenson State
    Park, 94–95
Robert Mondavi Winery, 76–77
Spring Lake County Park,
    104–105
Yountville City Park and Napa
    Valley, 109–111

San Francisco
Angel Island State Park, 36–37
Clipper Cove, Treasure Island–
    Yerba Buena, 17–18
Embarcadero Center, 152–153
Fort Point National Historic
    Site, 30–31
Palace of Fine Arts, 148–149
Rhododendron Dell, Golden
    Gate Park, 137–138
Sutro Heights Park, 15–16

San Mateo County
Coyote Point County Park,
    33–34
James V. Fitzgerald Marine
    Reserve, 51
Sam McDonald County Park,
    140–141
San Gregorio Beach State Park,
    120–121
San Mateo County Memorial
    Park, 165–166

Index of
Places and Recipes